easy peasy

easy peasy

Real cooking for kids who want to eat

Mary Contini & Pru Irvine

EBURY
PRESS
LONDON

This book is dedicated to all children who want to cook, and especially to Francesca, Lewis, Henry and Olivia.

First published in 1999

2 3 4 5 6 7 8 9 10

Text © Mary Contini and Pru Irvine 1999
Photographs © Ebury Press 1999

First published in the United Kingdom in 1999 by Ebury Press
Random House, 20 Vauxhall Bridge Road, London SW1V 2SA

Random House Australia (Pty) Limited
20 Alfred Street, Milsons Point, Sydney,
New South Wales 2061, Australia

Random House New Zealand Limited
18 Poland Road, Glenfield, Auckland 10, New Zealand

Random House South Africa (Pty) Limited
Endulina, 5a Jubilee Road, Parktown 2193, South Africa

Random House UK Limited Reg. No. 954009

Papers used by Ebury Press are natural, recyclable products made from wood grown in sustainable forests.

A CIP catalogue record for this book is available from the British Library.

ISBN 0 09 186840 8

Project editor Gillian Haslam
Designed by Redpath
Food photography by Philip Webb
Food styling by Dagmar Vasely

Printed and bound in Spain by Graficas Estella

Contents

Two Bossy Ladies

This is the story of two very bossy, very busy, noisy ladies who threw things into saucepans, stirred them once and produced dinner for twenty. They lived at opposite ends of the same city and had no idea of the other's existence.

Mary lived in a white house with two daughters and a husband who never stopped singing. The girls weren't easy to feed because they liked different things. The big one wanted only vegetables and garlic. The little one just wanted everything, all the time. They were a very Italian family. So there was lots of pasta and pizza and throwing of arms in the air. Mary owned a food shop and spent all day eating what her customers didn't buy.

Pru, on the other hand, lived in a brick house with a giant for a husband and two small giants for sons. Her husband didn't speak much but she and the boys never shut up. Theirs was a very noisy household. During the day she wrote stories. At night she dreamt about food.

Mary and Pru shared three things – they loved eating, cooking and children, in that order. They happened on each other by chance at a banquet hosted by a mutual friend, Soapy – a great bubble of a woman who collected friends like precious jewels. They sat next to each other at a table for 250 ladies who'd come to dinner to talk about food. They were each surprised to discover how bossy the other one was. Mary and Pru thought they had each found their match. And during the course of the evening they also discovered their shared passions.

Over the next few months they talked and ate and argued together as if they'd been friends for years. They talked about food. They ate their words and they argued about what young people could and could not do in the kitchen. But they were also sad. Sad that young people were no longer encouraged to cook. And sad that young people no longer thought of eating and cooking as a great pleasure and a lot of fun.

'I know,' shrieked Mary, 'We'll write a book!'

'A really easy peasy one,' said Pru with a big, cheesy grin.

So they set to with plans and proposals, ideas and recipes. And when they couldn't think of anything else to put in the book, they made themselves a cup of tea and thought about what to do next. Mary knew a very nice lady in London called Fiona.

'Fiona will know what to do,' she said. And sure as eggs is eggs, she did.

'I know,' said Fiona, 'We'll make a book. A really easy peasy one.'

And that's how this book came to be. So Pru and Mary are very grateful to Fiona, as they are to everyone who helped them make such an easy peasy book.

Pru Irvine (left) and Mary Contini

Dear Easy peasies

This book is for you. Why? Because you deserve it. Anyone who wants to cook deserves a cookery book of their own. Children's cookery books are often too babyish. Adult ones are too hard and too fancy. So make sure you keep this one away from all the other cookery books in your house. You know the ones, either crammed with complicated recipes for things like cows stuffed with pigs, stuffed with green vegetables and then sprinkled with vitamins. Or how to make a Swiss roll look like a witch with green snot. Ghastly.

If you catch an adult reading this book, be kind. They may also want to learn to cook absolutely fabulous, incredibly simple and gorgeous food. Let's face it – eating is brilliant. It's convenient. You can do it anytime and anywhere. (You can even dream about it.) It's fun. You can do it with anyone or anything. We don't care what people say about too much this and too much that and not enough A, B, C and D. Cooking and eating is good for you.

You see, we think we need a bit of everything. Chocolate and chips, chicken and chutney, peaches and peas. If you want cheese and marmalade, so be it. So remember, if you've time for school and television and sport and sleeping, then you've time for a little bit of Easy Peasy cooking – haven't you? Yes!

Love

Pru x & Mary x

P.S. We forgot to say all the recipes in Easy Peasy are really easy peasy. That's why they're in this book. Once you've cooked one or two, you'll discover you can cook three or four. Then suddenly, you'll find you can cook them all and still have time to watch television.

Dear Grown-ups

We're sorry but you can't have this book. It's for the children. And remember what we always say to children? 'You can't have everything you want.' If you can still behave like a child, you may be able to borrow it. But we've told them – Easy Peasy is theirs. So be warned.

We think eating is one of life's great pleasures, especially eating something fab you've cooked yourself. And the trouble with cooking for children is just that – adults trying to disguise foods so children will eat them. We want children to cook for themselves. For their friends. For you. That's what Easy Peasy is about – children cooking by themselves with a minimum amount of adult supervision. Lots of our recipes require no help at all, so you can put your feet up.

However, should you be tempted to try one or two or even three, you may find the children want to make them themselves anyway: 'Aw!' they'll say, 'This is gorgeous. What is it?' 'Well dear,' you can say, 'It's really very easy peasy. You can make it for me next week. It's in your book.'

Cooking is also a life skill. Once you know the basics you can survive anywhere. And with school meals under the microscope it's even more important for children to know about the pleasures of eating well and the problems of eating badly. It's just another way of helping them towards a strong and healthy adult-hood. School may take care of reading, writing and arithmetic, but strong bones and strong bodies come from us.

Apart from anything else, you may hate cooking. Maybe you love it but haven't got the time. There are loads of reasons why so many of us don't cook. But children love cooking. It makes them feel proud and gives them a sense of sharing and achievement. So encourage them.

With best wishes,

Pru x & Mary x

Inside Easy peasy

Excuse me, could we just say something before you start reading? You know how sometimes a recipe asks you to do something that you've not done before? Or even something that you think you should know how to do but don't? Well it's all in the **Easy Peasy How To Do Everything Brilliantly** section starting on page 12. So suppose you need to know something about carrots – chopping, slicing, peeling or grating – just turn to that section and find carrots.

And if we mention a piece of equipment that you're not sure you have, just look in the **Easy Peasy Pots and Pans** section on page 18. It's really easy peasy.

Easy Peasy cooking means being prepared. Get everything ready before you start cooking. Always check with an adult if you need to use sharp knives or the cooker.

By the way, all the recipes will feed four of you unless we tell you otherwise.

Spoons: tablespoon = a soup spoon
dessertspoon = a pudding spoon
teaspoon = a teaspoon

Can sizes: small = about 220g
medium = about 420g

An **ovenproof** dish means a dish that can be put into a hot oven and will not crack.

Easy peasy How to do Everything Brilliantly

'Waiter! Waiter! Has this lettuce been washed?'
'Yes Sir, you can still see the soap on it!'

This section tells you how to prepare, wash, peel and chop vegetables and fruit.

Apples

If you need to **peel** and **core** an apple, use a sharp knife and a chopping board. Cut the apple in half and then into quarters. Using the knife, trim away the hard core and the pips in the middle of each quarter and carefully peel them. It's best to peel apples just before you need them because they go brown if they're left to hang around without any skin on.

Avocados

These are easy to prepare if they're **ripe**. Take a sharp knife and cut through the skin from top to bottom all the way around. Gently **twist** the two halves in opposite directions until they come apart. Pull the stone out. It's very **slippery** and you sometimes have to push your fingers into the flesh to loosen it. Then peel off the skin and chop or slice as needed.

Broccoli

Using a sharp knife, cut off as much broccoli as you need using both the dark green **fuzzy bits** at the top and the bits of **stalk** that go with them. Rinse well under cold running water.

Carrots

Using a sharp knife, **slice off** both ends. Hold the thick end of the carrot with one hand and with the other use, a vegetable peeler to **peel** down towards the bottom of the carrot. Keep turning it round in your hand until all the skin is gone. Then rinse the carrot in cold water. Be careful **chopping** carrots as they have a way of sliding around. You can slice the carrot into rounds or cut lengthways into two and then four, depending on the size of the carrot.

Celery

Celery always needs a good, thorough wash under cold running water. When you need to **chop** it, use a sharp knife and cut off the leaves first. Take a small **slice** off each end and run the vegetable peeler down the length of the celery. This gets rid of all those horrid, stringy bits.

Cucumber

Cut yourself a chunk using a sharp knife and peel away the dark green skin. If you want to peel a whole cucumber, it's great fun to use a vegetable peeler, slicing from top to bottom.

Eggs

Separating the yolk and the white is a messy job. You really need two bowls for each egg. Take an egg and **whack** the shell quite hard in its middle over the rim of a bowl. Holding the egg upright in one hand, push your **thumb** into the crack and gently prise apart the shell, keeping the yolk safely inside one half of the shell, while the white **drips** into the other bowl. Then, very gently, tip the yolk into the other half of the shell, allowing more of the egg white to drip into the bowl. You need to be careful not to get any yolk mixed up with the whites, or you won't be able to whisk them. Keep doing this carefully until all the white has dripped off. You never get it all but you'll get most of it. Pour the yolk into the second bowl.

Garlic Cloves

Using a sharp knife, **slice** off the top and bottom and **peel** away the outer skin. There's no need to wash garlic. You can **chop** it in lots of ways – very thin slices, tiny chunks or simply left whole.

Herbs

All fresh herbs (not the dried ones that come in jars) need to be **rinsed** in cold water and given a good shaking to dry them. When you need a 'handful', it means just that – as much as you can hold in one hand. **Squeeze** them into a ball as best you can and, on a chopping board, **cut** them up using a sharp knife. When you've done that, gather all the bits together again and cut them again until the herbs are chopped up small.

Mango

Everyone says mango is really difficult to peel. It's not true. It's easy peasy. Hold the mango firmly in one hand or on a board. **Cut** through the skin with a sharp knife from top to bottom. Do this about five times all around the mango so it looks like uncut segments. Then gently **pull** away a bit of skin at the top and when you've got a good hold on it, pull it all the way to the bottom. Do that for about three of the strips and then **cut** out the flesh around the stone. Keep going until all the skin and flesh is off. Mangoes do need to be soft to peel easily. This is also a good way to peel an orange.

Mushrooms

These are sometimes fairly dirty. If so, **rinse** them well in cold water to remove the mud and grit. If they are quite clean, simply **wipe** them with a piece of damp kitchen paper. Take a thin slice off the stalk end and throw it away. Then slice the mushrooms as required by the recipe.

Onions

To peel onions, use a sharp knife in one hand and hold the onion firmly with the other. **Slice** off the top and bottom and **peel** away the dry, papery outer skin. You may find it easier to cut the onion in half before peeling it. There's no need to wash onions after they've been peeled. Slicing onions means **cutting** each one into quarters first and then **slicing** across and down each quarter. Do this as thinly as you can manage. Any bits that fall away while you're cutting can just be chopped up at the end. Chopping onions means cutting the slices again into smaller pieces.

Oranges, Lemons and Limes

These are known as citrus fruits. When you're asked to **zest** an orange or lemon, it means peeling away tiny strips of the outer skin. You really need a zester for the job. To see what a zester looks like, turn to page 18. You could also do this, being very careful, using a vegetable peeler and then slicing the slithers very thinly with a sharp knife. Always wash these fruits in hot, soapy water before peeling or zesting to remove the wax on their skins (but be sure to rinse all the soapy water off too).

Pastry or Pizza Dough

Rolling out pastry or dough is not the easiest of jobs. Make sure you completely defrost the pastry if it is frozen. Here's how you **roll** it: use a clean board sprinkled with a little flour. Also sprinkle your rolling pin. If your pastry is in a heap or a ball then begin by pressing the rolling pin down into the middle and gently pushing away from you. Turn either the board or the pastry round and roll the pin over it again. Keep doing this until you've got the right shape. It's never perfect and it doesn't matter. Some-times you can even use your fingertips to press the pastry into the right shape. You can always sprinkle a little flour on to the pastry itself if it's getting too sticky.

Peppers

Slice off the stalk end and cut the pepper in half lengthways. **Rinse** out all the little white seeds under cold, running water and **pull** off any white bits of the flesh inside. Using a sharp knife, **slice** the pepper into slices about as thick as a pencil. If you need chunks, then cut chunks.

Potatoes

Rinse off any dirt under the cold tap. Hold the potato firmly in one hand and with the other, using a vegetable peeler, **peel** from the top to the bottom of the potato, turning it around until all the skin is off. Peeled potatoes are slippery so be extra careful when **chopping**.

Root Ginger

Cut off a chunk the size you need. **Scrub** it in cold water and slice it as thinly as you can with a sharp knife.

Soft Fruits

Raspberries and strawberries can be **rinsed** gently in cold water just before use. When rinsing raspberries, look out for little insects which like to hide inside. The simplest way to take the stalk off a strawberry is to **slice** it off with a sharp knife. Always cut off any mouldy bits.

Spring onions

Using a sharp knife, first **cut** off most of the dark green bits and then take a tiny **slice** off the other end where the roots are. **Rinse** them under cold water, pulling away any loose bits of outer skin. Chopping spring onions just means slicing them thinly after you've peeled and washed them.

How to Work it Out

'What kinds of dogs hide from frying pans?'
'Sausage dogs!'

Boiling

This just means liquid that's hot enough to **bubble** fast.

Food Processors

These are great things. They do everything: **grate**, **chop**, **mix**, **knead**. If you've got one, then ask to be shown how to use it.

Frying

This is hot work. It means cooking something in oil or butter that's hot enough to **sizzle**. Always use long-handled utensils as hot oil and butter can spit at you. Be careful.

Grating

You can either grate in the **food processor**, using the grating attachment, or **by hand**. If you do it by hand, hold the grater firmly in one hand, resting it on a board. With the other hand, press the food you're going to grate against the top of the grater and slide it up and down. Be careful not to skin your knuckles when you get close to the end. To help protect your knuckles it's often helpful to hold a clean tea towel around whatever you're grating.

Greasing

This is a nice job. Lots of recipes need a greased tin, baking sheet or dish. If you're using oil, simply **pour** a little into the dish and, using a piece of kitchen paper, **rub** the oil all over the inside of the dish, remembering the edges and the corners. If using butter, take a blob of soft butter on a piece of kitchen paper and do the same. Greasing stops the food sticking to the dish while it is cooking.

Grilling

This usually means using a grill with a grilling pan and cooking under an overhead heat. It's a good way of cooking with very little **fat** because grill pans let fat drip off the grilling rack and into the pan.

Kneading

This is great fun but requires patience. Make sure you sprinkle a little flour on the surface you will be using. Flour your own hands as well. Put the dough on the board or work surface and using the heel of your hand (the flat bit attached to your wrist), **push down** into the dough and away from you. **Fold** the dough over any way you like and repeat. Keep doing this until the dough feels like the recipe says it should feel. It takes a bit of time and is quite tiring. You don't need to show it any respect at all. Use all your muscles and just go for it. If the dough starts sticking to your hands or the board, sprinkle a little more flour over them and the board. Alternatively, if you have a **food processor** with a dough hook (the white plastic blade), use that. It takes only a few minutes to knead dough this way and should be done on a moderate or fast speed.

Liquidising

This is easy peasy – if you've got a liquidiser. To see what they look like turn to page 20. Basically all you do is **pile** all the ingredients in, taking care not to overfill it, put on the lid, and turn on. Keep **whizzing** until whatever you're making is the right thickness or smoothness. Sometimes you need to stop the liquidiser and push the ingredients down with a wooden spoon or a spatula so they all get mashed up.

Making More

Sometimes a recipe is for two people and you want to cook for four. Just **double** all the quantities. Double them as though you're cooking for two or four or six or eight and so on. It's too difficult judging quantities for three or five or seven people. Stick to your two-times table!

Simmering

This means liquid hot enough to bubble **gently** and slowly.

whisking

This is quite hard work. You usually whisk eggs or cream. It's a way of **mixing very fast**, often to combine watery liquids, to mix a yolk with its white, to make cream stiff or to remove lumps. You can use an ordinary fork for whisking but some people prefer a whisk. To see what a hand whisk and an electric whisk look like, turn to pages 19 and 21.

Easy peasy pots & pans

Rolling pin

potato ma[sher]

Garlic crusher

Ladle

Tongs

zester

vegetable peeler

Serrated kni[fe]

Sharp knife

Spatula

Ramekins

Grater

Whisk

Pastry cutter

Orange juicer

Tea strainer

Pastry brush

Skewer

Easy peasy pots & pans

Liquidiser/blender

Grill pan

Cooling wire rack

Sieve

PHILIPS

Food processor

Electric wand or hand-held blender

potatoes

Before you begin:

- Easy Peasy means being prepared. Get everything ready before you start cooking.

- Each recipe serves 4 people, unless we tell you otherwise.

- If the recipe tells you to do something you don't understand, look back at the sections on 'Easy Peasy Pots and Pans' (page 18) and 'How To Do Everything Brilliantly' (page 12).

- Remember to take care when using sharp knives and always use oven gloves when taking dishes in and out of the oven.

- When you have finished cooking, always remember to turn off the oven, cooker or grill.

Mash Them Up

For 2 people

You will need:

2 large potatoes
cold water
2 level teaspoons of salt
3 tablespoons of milk
a big blob of butter

a vegetable peeler
a chopping board
a sharp knife
a saucepan big enough to hold
* all the potatoes*
a colander, placed in the sink
a teaspoon
a tablespoon
a potato masher
oven gloves

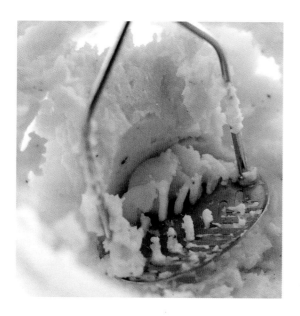

1. Wash the potatoes in cold water and peel them. Rinse them again.
2. On the chopping board cut each one into four pieces.
3. Put them in the saucepan with enough cold water to cover them.
4. Add the salt and taste the water. It should be salty.
5. Put the saucepan on the cooker and turn the heat on high. As soon as the water begins to bubble, turn the heat down and leave the potatoes to cook slowly with the water bubbling gently.
6. After about 15 minutes they should be cooked. Test them by pushing the sharp knife into one of them. If it slides in easily, they're ready. If not, cook them for a little longer.
7. Using the oven gloves, take the saucepan to the sink and pour the potatoes into the colander to drain away all the water.
8. Put the potatoes back in the saucepan and add the milk and butter. Mash them well until they're soft and fluffy. Taste them and if you feel they need more salt, butter or milk, then add it.

EASY PEASY TOO
OVEN-BAKED CHEESY MASH

Turn on the oven to 175°C/350°F/gas mark 4. Mix 3 tablespoons of grated Cheddar cheese into the mashed potatoes. Put them into an ovenproof dish, sprinkle more cheese on the top and add a couple of blobs of butter. Bake in the oven for 15 minutes until the cheese melts and becomes crisp around the edges.

Spud pie

You will need:

5 large baking potatoes
2 medium sized onions
2 eggs
salt and pepper
2 tablespoons of plain flour
plenty of butter

a vegetable peeler
a grater
a large and small bowl
a chopping board
a sharp knife
a fork
a tablespoon
kitchen paper
an ovenproof dish
oven gloves

1. Turn on the oven to 180°C/350°F/ gas mark 4.
2. Wash the potatoes in the sink in cold water and peel them.
3. Grate them into large shreds. (If you've got a food processor with a grating attachment, use that.)
4. With clean hands, squeeze all the water out of the potatoes and put them into the large bowl.
5. Peel the onions and chop them into very small pieces.
6. Break the eggs into the small bowl, add some salt and pepper and whisk them with the fork.
7. Add the onions, eggs and flour to the potatoes and mix everything well.
8. Put some butter on a piece of kitchen paper and rub it all over the ovenproof dish. Be extra careful to butter the corners well.
9. Pile the potato mixture into the dish and spread it out evenly. Dot a few more blobs of butter on top.
10. Using your oven gloves, put the dish into the oven and cook it for about 1½ hours until the top is crisp and brown.

Potato wedges

For 2 people

Easy Peasy Potato Wedges are great on their own or with a good dollop of tomato ketchup or mayonnaise.

You will need:

2 large potatoes
vegetable or olive oil
a big pinch of salt

kitchen paper
a baking dish
a vegetable peeler
a chopping board
a sharp knife
a bowl of cold water
a tablespoon
a small bowl
oven gloves
a spatula

1. Turn on the oven to 220ºC/440ºF/ gas mark 7.
2. Oil the baking dish.
3. Wash the potatoes in cold water. Peel them with the vegetable peeler.
4. Cut each one into four pieces lengthways, making long wedges.
Put them into the bowl of cold water.
5. Put three tablespoons of oil and the salt into the small bowl.

6. Dry the wedges with kitchen paper and rub them all over in the oil. Lay them in the baking dish and using your oven gloves, pop them onto the middle shelf of the oven.
7. After about 20 minutes and using your oven gloves, take the dish out of the oven and place it on a surface that will not be damaged by the heat.
8. Using the spatula, turn the wedges over and, using your oven gloves, put them back into the oven for another 10 minutes.
9. Take them out again and using your gloves and being careful, check they're cooked by pushing the sharp knife into one or two. They should be crisp on the outside but soft inside. Cook them a little longer if they still seem hard.

EASY PEASY TOO PUMPKIN STICKS

Follow the same recipe using pumpkin instead of potatoes. You may need more oil. Buy pumpkins that are small and very orange. They are quite difficult to cut so you may need help. Cut the pumpkin in half and take out the seeds and the woolly fibres from the middle. Use the vegetable peeler or a sharp knife to remove the skin. You can cut the flesh into sticks or cubes.

packed potatoes

You will need:

4 medium sized baking potatoes
4 slices of smoked ham
about 4 tablespoons of grated Cheddar
   cheese
lots of butter
2 tablespoons of mayonnaise or crème
   fraîche
a handful of finely chopped fresh parsley
   or chives
salt

kitchen paper or a tea towel
a skewer
a baking tray big enough to hold the
   potatoes
oven gloves
a bowl
a sharp knife
a spoon
a fork
a chopping board

1. Turn on the oven to 220°C/425°F/
gas mark 7.
2. Wash the potatoes in cold water,
scrubbing off any dirt. Dry them with
kitchen paper or a tea towel.
3. Using the skewer, pierce the skin of
each potato two or three times and put
them on the baking tray.
4. Using your oven gloves, pop the baking
tray onto the middle shelf of the oven and
leave them for 1 hour.
5. Then, using your oven gloves, take
them out of the oven and test to see if

they're cooked by pushing the skewer into
the biggest. If it goes in easily they're ready.
If not, put them back into the oven for
another 15 minutes or so. Test again.
6. Meanwhile, tear the ham into small shreds
and mix it with the cheese, butter, mayonnaise
and herbs. Put it all into the bowl.
7. When the potatoes are cooked, hold each
one with an oven glove and slice the top off.
8. Using a fork or a spoon, scoop out the
potato into the bowl.
9. Mix everything together and add some
salt. Taste it to check it's good and then pile
it back into the empty potato skins and put
the lids back on.
10. Pop them back into the oven for another
10 minutes.

EASY PEASY TOO

You can pack potatoes with anything you like.
Always remember to taste the filling after
you've mixed everything. Add more salt or
butter if you want.
• Try mixing 2 chopped, hard-boiled eggs
with 4 tablespoons of double cream and
some salt and pepper.
• Gently fry some chopped up bacon and
some sliced mushrooms in a little butter
in a frying pan. Let it cool, then mix it with
a little butter and add it to the potato filling.
• Mix 4 tablespoons of cream cheese with
1 tablespoon of chopped spring onions and
1 tablespoon of chutney. Mix it with a little
butter and add it to the potato filling.

Potato Bangers

You will need:

2 large onions
5 medium sized potatoes
2 tablespoons of vegetable oil
6 pork or beef sausages
1 dessertspoon of Worcestershire sauce
salt
hot water from the kettle
brown sauce or tomato ketchup

a vegetable peeler
a chopping board
a sharp knife
a medium sized bowl
a medium sized saucepan with a lid
a wooden spoon
a teaspoon

1. Peel the onions, cut them into quarters and slice them as thinly as you can.
2. Peel the potatoes, cut them into medium sized chunks and put them into a bowl of cold water until you need them (this stops them going black).
3. Put the saucepan on the cooker on a medium heat.
4. Add the oil to the saucepan and allow it to warm through. Now add the onions, stir them around with the wooden spoon and cook them gently and slowly until they're soft and clear.

5. Cut the sausages into chunks and add them to the onions. Turn up the heat and cook them until they're brown all over.
6. Now drain the potatoes, add them to the sausages with the Worcestershire sauce and just enough hot water from the kettle to cover half of them. Give it a good stir.
7. Put the lid on and cook on a medium heat until the potatoes are completely soft and mushy.
8. Check them now and then and add a little more water if they get too dry. Don't worry if some of the potatoes stick to the bottom of the pan. They will still taste very good.
9. Check they've got enough salt and serve them piping hot with brown sauce or tomato ketchup.

EASY PEASY TOO

• Try adding some frozen peas for the last 5 minutes.
• You could also serve this recipe with a tin of baked beans.

Square Chips

Ask an adult to help the first time you try this recipe.

You will need:

4 or 5 medium sized potatoes
vegetable oil
salt

a vegetable peeler
a chopping board
a sharp knife
a plate with some kitchen paper
a large frying pan
a large slotted spoon

1. Wash the potatoes in the sink in cold water and peel them. Rinse them, cut them into cubes and lay them on kitchen paper to dry.
2. Add enough oil in the frying pan to come half way up the sides. Add one potato cube and when it starts to sizzle, the oil is hot enough.
3. Now add about 3 tablespoons of cubes and keep them sizzling, turning them over with the slotted spoon to brown them all over. Be careful of the hot oil which can spit.
4. When they're crisp and golden take them out of the pan and drain them on some fresh kitchen paper. Keep them somewhere warm, such as in the oven.
5. Add the rest of the potatoes to the oil in batches and cook them the same way.

Gold Fish Cakes

Ask an adult to help the first time you try this recipe. They're absolutely gorgeous with *Easy Peasy Saucy Salsa* (see page 82).

You will need:

3 medium sized potatoes
salt and pepper
about 250g of undyed, smoked haddock
     fillets (you can use unsmoked, ordinary
     white fillets if you prefer)
some butter
some milk
1 bay leaf
a tablespoon of chopped fresh parsley
some plain flour
about 8 tablespoons of vegetable oil
     for frying

a vegetable peeler
a chopping board
a sharp knife
2 medium sized saucepans
a teaspoon
a sieve or colander
a potato masher
a medium sized bowl
a tablespoon
2 plates
a frying pan
a spatula
a serving plate and kitchen paper

1. Wash the potatoes in the sink in cold water and peel them. Cut them into quarters and put them into a saucepan.
2. Cover them with cold water, add a teaspoon of salt and boil them for 15-20 minutes until they're cooked. To test whether they're cooked, push the sharp knife into one or two of them. If it goes in easily they're ready. If not, cook them a bit longer.
3. When they're ready, drain them in the colander and mash them well with a little butter and about 4 tablespoons of milk. Put them into a bowl.
4. Now press the fish all over with your fingers to make sure there are no bones. If you find any, use the knife to cut them out. Don't worry if the fish breaks up.
5. Wash the fish and cut it so it fits into the second saucepan. Add the bay leaf, enough milk or water to cover the fish and a little salt. Slowly, using a medium heat, bring it to the boil (keep an eye on it as milk boils over very quickly).
6. Now lower the heat and cook the fish gently for about 15 minutes. Leave it to cool and then drain it. Throw out the bay leaf.
7. Flake the fish into the mashed potatoes, add the parsley and mix everything together.
8. Taste it and add more salt and pepper if you want.
9. Put some flour onto a plate and season it with some salt and pepper.
10. Wash your hands and dry them well. Dust them with some plain flour.

11. Take about a tablespoon of the mixture at a time and roll it into balls. Pat them to flatten them a little and dip them into the flour. Lay them on the plate, ready to be cooked.

12. Wash your hands again.

13. Heat the oil in the frying pan and add a tiny piece of the mixture. When it starts to sizzle, add about 4 fish cakes. Be careful because they can splash and spit.

14. When they are brown on the underside, turn them over using the spatula. They need about 2 minutes on each side.

15. Drain them on kitchen paper before eating.

EASY PEASY TOO

You can add lots of flavourings to make these taste even better.

• Try adding different herbs, such as fresh, chopped coriander with some chopped garlic.

• For a much stronger flavour, add 2 chopped anchovies and a teaspoon of chopped capers.

eggs

Before you begin:

- Easy Peasy means being prepared. Get everything ready before you start cooking.

- Each recipe serves 4 people, unless we tell you otherwise.

- If the recipe tells you to do something you don't understand, look back at the sections on 'Easy Peasy Pots and Pans' (page 18) and 'How To Do Everything Brilliantly' (page 12).

- Remember to take care when using sharp knives and always use oven gloves when taking dishes in and out of the oven.

- When you have finished cooking, always remember to turn off the oven, cooker or grill.

Dipping Soldiers

For each person you will need:

2 fresh eggs
water

a small saucepan
a tablespoon
an egg timer or clock

1. If the eggs have been kept in the fridge put them in the saucepan with enough cold water to cover them and bring them to the boil. If they've been kept out of the fridge, bring the water to the boil first and gently lower the eggs into it, using the tablespoon.

2. As soon as the water starts to boil, time the eggs like this:

Medium egg: soft-boiled: 4 minutes
              hard-boiled: 7 minutes
Large egg: soft-boiled: 5 minutes
              hard-boiled: 8 minutes

You'll quickly learn how long to cook your egg to your own taste. Use these times as a guideline.

To check whether an egg is hard-boiled, lift it out of the saucepan and if the water evaporates quickly and leaves the shell looking dry, then you'll know it's cooked properly. If the egg is still soft inside, the shell will stay wet longer. Always run cold water over a cooked hard-boiled egg until it cools down. This stops it cooking longer.

If you're not sure whether an egg is hard-boiled or raw, spin it on a flat surface. Place your finger on it to stop it moving and then take it off immediately. If the egg is raw it will continue to spin.

Now for the SOLDIERS

For each person you will need:

2 slices of white or brown bread
some soft butter

a toaster
a knife
a chopping board

1. Toast the bread in the toaster until brown.
2. Butter it and, using the chopping board, slice each piece into four or five long strips to dip into your eggs.

Flat in the pan

For each person you will need:

2 eggs
salt and pepper
a blob of butter

a small bowl
a whisk
a small non-stick frying pan
a spatula

1. Break the eggs into the bowl. Add a little salt and pepper and whisk them well.
2. Melt the butter in the frying pan over a medium heat.
3. Add the eggs and stir them around using the whisk so they cover the whole surface of the frying pan.
4. Leave them alone for about 4 minutes until the bottom of the egg begins to get firm.
5. Fold the omelette in half with the spatula and let it cook for another 2 or 3 minutes until there's no more liquid.
6. Tip it onto your plate and eat.

EASY PEASY TOO

To change flavours try adding some of these ingredients as soon as the egg gets firm and before you fold it over:
• 2 tablespoons of grated Cheddar or Jarlsberg cheese
• A few strips of chopped ham and some sliced mushrooms
• Some chopped tomatoes
• Some cold cooked potatoes, chopped up with some fresh mint leaves
• If you want to add onions, which taste wonderful, cook them in a little butter before you start the omelette. Slice a small onion thinly and cook in a blob of butter until it's soft and browning. Add them half way through cooking the omelette.

Eggy Pots

Ask an adult to help the first time you try this recipe.

For each person you will need:

soft butter
2 eggs
salt and pepper
2 tablespoons of milk

2 ramekins (small ovenproof dishes)
kitchen paper
a tablespoon
a roasting tin
a kettle of hot water
oven gloves

1. Turn on the oven to 190°C/375°F/ gas mark 5.
2. Using kitchen paper, rub the ramekins all over the inside with plenty of butter.
3. Break an egg into each ramekin. Add a little salt and pepper and a tablespoon of milk. Pop a little blob of butter on top of each one.
4. Using your oven gloves, put them into the roasting tin and pour the hot water into the tin until it comes half way up the ramekins.
5. Ask an adult to help you put the roasting tin onto the middle shelf of the oven.
6. Cook for about 15 minutes and ask for some help to take them out of the oven.
7. Let them cool a bit before eating them.

EASY PEASY TOO

• Try adding some tomatoes, chopped into tiny bits and popped into the ramekin with the egg before you cook it.
• You could also add a little grated cheese, either in with the egg or sprinkled on top.

Scrabble

For each person you will need:

2 eggs
2 tablespoons of milk
salt and pepper
a blob of butter

a small bowl
a tablespoon
a fork
a small saucepan
a wooden spoon

1. Break the eggs into the bowl, add the milk and a little salt and pepper.
2. Whisk them together with the fork.
3. Melt the butter in the saucepan over a medium heat.
4. Turn the heat up high and add the eggs. Cook them really quickly using the wooden spoon to stir them around and stop them sticking. They will only take about 3 minutes.
5. Eat them right away as they do continue cooking for a while after they've come off the heat.

EASY PEASY TOO

• Add a tablespoon of grated Cheddar cheese to the egg mixture to make cheesy scrabble.
• Add some thin slices of smoked salmon to the eggs as you cook them. This is extra lovely with some chopped fresh dill.

Corn Critters

Ask an adult to help the first time you try this recipe.

For 2 people

You will need:

2 large eggs
2 tablespoons of self-raising flour
2 tablespoons of milk
a tin of strained sweetcorn (about 225g)
salt and pepper
about 6-8 tablespoons of corn or vegetable oil

a medium sized bowl
a sieve
a fork
a frying pan
a tablespoon
a spatula
a serving plate and kitchen paper

1. Break the eggs into the bowl, sieve in the flour and add the milk. Mix them together really well with the fork.
2. Add the sweetcorn and a little salt and pepper. Mix again.
3. Heat the oil in the frying pan. Add a tiny drop of the sweetcorn batter and when it sizzles the oil is hot enough.
4. Put three separate tablespoons of the batter into the frying pan to make three pancakes. Cook them for about 3 minutes until they start to look firm and brown on their bottoms. (If the oil is spitting at you, turn down the heat a little.)
5. Using the spatula, turn them over and cook the other side for a couple of minutes.
6. Drain them on the kitchen paper and keep in a warm place, such as the oven, while you cook all the rest the same way.

Corn Critters – alternatives

SPRING ONION PANCAKES

Make the same mixture but use about 6 spring onions (cleaned and finely chopped) instead of sweetcorn. Flavour them with a teaspoon of soya sauce and some fresh ginger that has been chopped into tiny bits.

SWEET BANANA PANCAKES

Instead of salt and pepper and sweetcorn add 2 teaspoons of sugar and 2 or 3 sliced bananas to the mixture. Sprinkle them with a little caster sugar before serving.

Greece Salad

For 2 people

You will need:

2 hard-boiled eggs (see page 36)
3 tomatoes, cut into little chunks
8 stoned black olives
a chunk of peeled and cubed cucumber
100g Greek feta cheese, cut into chunks

For the dressing:
3 tablespoons of olive oil
1 tablespoon of lemon juice
1 teaspoon Dijon mustard
a little pepper

a chopping board
a sharp knife
a vegetable peeler
a medium sized bowl
a jar with a lid, to put the dressing in
tablespoons
a teaspoon

1. Shell the eggs and cut them into quarters.
2. Add all the ingredients to the bowl and mix them around gently.
3. Put all the dressing ingredients into the jar, put the lid on and shake.
4. Pour the dressing over the salad and mix together.
5. Taste the salad and add a bit of salt if you need it. Feta cheese is quite salty.

EASY PEASY TOO

Try this dressing instead:

• A squeeze of lemon juice and 2 or 3 tablespoons of mayonnaise. Use this to fill a large crunchy baguette which has been slit down the middle.

pasta

Before you begin:

- Easy Peasy means being prepared. Get everything ready before you start cooking.

- Each recipe serves 4 people, unless we tell you otherwise.

- If the recipe tells you to do something you don't understand, look back at the sections on 'Easy Peasy Pots and Pans' (page 18) and 'How To Do Everything Brilliantly' (page 12).

- Remember to take care when using sharp knives and always use oven gloves when taking dishes in and out of the oven.

- When you have finished cooking, always remember to turn off the oven, cooker or grill.

Cooking pasta

Always have the pasta sauce ready before you cook the pasta. Pasta doesn't like to wait for its sauce.

You will need:

100g of pasta for each person
salt

a large saucepan, no lid
a teaspoon
a long-handled spoon
a fork
oven gloves
a colander in the sink

1. Fill the saucepan three-quarters full with cold water. Bring it to the boil over a high heat.
2. Add about 4 teaspoons of salt. Carefully taste the water which needs to be quite salty (remember the water will be hot, so let it cool on a spoon for a minute before you taste it).
3. Add the pasta to the saucepan and use the long-handled spoon to stir it so it doesn't stick together.
4. Check the packet for cooking times. Most pasta takes between 4 and 12 minutes. Using the fork, carefully take a piece out of the pot and taste it. Remember it will be very hot. If it seems too hard, then cook it for another minute. Keep trying it until it's cooked and has a nice bite to it.
5. Using the oven gloves, take the saucepan to the sink and drain the pasta into the colander, then tip it back into the saucepan.
6. Have the hot sauce ready and add it to the pasta. Stir it around and serve immediately.

Cooking Rice

You will need:

half a cup of easy-cook rice per person
salt

cup
a saucepan with a lid
a sieve
a fork

1. You need twice as much water as rice. Use the cups for measuring – one cup of rice needs two cups of water.
2. Pour the water into the saucepan and bring it to the boil. Add enough salt so it tastes salty.
3. Rinse the rice in the sieve under cold running water and add it to the boiling water. Give it a stir and bring it back to the boil.
4. Lower the heat and put on the lid. Cook the rice on a very low heat for about 10 minutes.
5. The rice should soak up all the water. Fluff it up with the fork when it's cooked.

EASY PEASY TOO

• Try adding a tablespoon of mango chutney to the boiled rice.

Quicky Saucey

You will need:

3 tablespoons of olive oil
1 clove of garlic, peeled and chopped
a medium tin of chopped tomatoes
    (about 425g)
a handful of fresh basil
some salt

a saucepan, no lid
a sharp knife
a chopping board
a wooden spoon

1. Add the oil to the saucepan and warm it over a low heat.
2. Add the garlic and cook it slowly for 3-4 minutes, stirring it with the wooden spoon. Don't let it burn.
3. Add the tomatoes and the basil.
4. Stir it around and cook gently for about 20 minutes.
5. Add some salt and taste it. Add more if you want.
6. Serve this with pasta. It's especially good with long spaghetti.

EASY PEASY TOO

• You can use this sauce as a pizza topping or for *Drizzle Toast* on page 88.

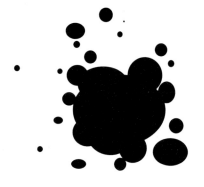

Not-so-Quicky Saucey

You will need:

4 tablespoons of olive oil
1 clove of garlic, peeled and finely chopped
1 small onion, finely chopped
1 carrot, peeled and finely chopped
1 stick of celery, finely chopped
2 tins of chopped tomatoes
  (about 425g each)
some salt
a handful of fresh basil
grated Parmesan cheese

a saucepan with a lid
a sharp knife
a vegetable peeler
a chopping board
a wooden spoon

1. Warm the olive oil in the saucepan over a low heat.
2. Add the garlic, stir with the wooden spoon and leave for a minute or so.
3. Now add the onion, carrot and celery. Stir them well and cook them very slowly until they're soft and clear. This will take about 15 minutes.
4. Add the tomatoes and let them cook gently. Partly cover the saucepan with the lid to allow some steam to escape.
5. Cook for about 45 minutes.
6. Add some salt and some fresh basil leaves.
7. Use this sauce for chunky pasta and sprinkle it with some grated Parmesan cheese.

EASY PEASY TOO

• Add another layer of flavour with some chopped bacon or some sliced, spicy Italian sausage just before you add the carrot and celery.
• Make an Easy Peasy Bolognese by adding 300g of lean minced beef after you've softened the vegetables. Turn the heat up high. Brown the meat, add salt and then the tomatoes. Cook the sauce very slowly for about 1½ hours with the saucepan lid half on and half off.

Pig and Fungus Sauce

You will need:

a blob of butter
1 clove of garlic, finely chopped
1 small onion, very finely chopped
150g of button mushrooms, washed
    and thinly sliced
150g of smoked ham, cut into strips
    or cubes
a tin of chopped tomatoes (about 425g)
1 tablespoon of chopped, fresh parsley
some salt

a saucepan with a lid
a wooden spoon
a sharp knife
a chopping board

1. Melt the butter in the saucepan over a low heat.
2. Add the garlic and cook it until it begins to smell garlicky. Stir it with a wooden spoon while cooking it.
3. Add the onion and stir. Cook it very gently for about 10 minutes.
4. Add the mushrooms and allow them to cook for another 10 minutes.
5. Add the ham, the tomatoes and the parsley.
6. Let the sauce cook gently for about 30 minutes with the lid half on.
7. Add some salt and check the flavour.
8. Serve this sauce with chunky pasta.

Nice Rice

You will need:

2 tablespoons of olive oil
1 clove of garlic, peeled and finely
    chopped
1 small onion, peeled and finely chopped
2 sticks of celery, peeled and finely
    chopped
a small tin of chopped tomatoes (about
    220g)
a gammon steak, cut into cubes
350g of 'pre-cooked' rice
1 ham stock cube dissolved in 600ml
    of boiling water
some fresh basil or parsley
grated Parmesan cheese

a tablespoon
a saucepan with a lid
a sharp knife
a chopping board
a wooden spoon
a heat-proof measuring jug
a kettle of boiling water

1. Warm the oil in the saucepan.
2. Add the garlic, onion and celery and stir them with the wooden spoon.
3. Allow the vegetables to cook slowly until they are soft. This will take about 5-10 minutes.
4. Add the tomatoes, the gammon and the rice to the saucepan and stir them around.
5. Add the hot stock.
6. Let the mixture cook gently with the lid on for about 25-30 minutes, stirring it now and then with the wooden spoon. Add some more hot water if it gets dry and starts to stick to the saucepan.
7. Add the fresh herbs and some salt and taste it. Serve it with some freshly grated Parmesan cheese sprinkled on top.

EASY PEASY TOO

• Instead of the gammon you can make this with chopped courgettes, peppers and mushrooms. Add about 300g of any vegetables you like.

picnic pasta

You will need:

250g of pasta twirls or other chunky pasta
2 tomatoes, washed and chopped into
    cubes
a chunk of cucumber, peeled and
    chopped
2 sticks celery, washed and chopped into
    tiny cubes
half a red pepper, de-seeded and chopped
1 spring onion, trimmed and sliced
a tablespoon of stoned black olives
lots of fresh chopped herbs: parsley,
basil or chives

For the dressing:

3 tablespoons of olive oil
1 teaspoon of Dijon mustard
the juice of half a lemon
a teaspoon of sugar
some salt and pepper

a saucepan
a colander
a large bowl
a sharp knife
a chopping board
a large spoon
a clean jam jar with a lid
a fork
a teaspoon

1. Boil the pasta (see page 48) and drain
it in the colander. Now tip it into the bowl.
2. Add all the vegetables, olives and herbs
and mix everything together.
3. To make the dressing, put all the dressing
ingredients into the jam jar, screw on the lid
and shake it up.
4. Add the dressing to the salad and mix it.
5. Taste the salad and add more salt and
pepper if you want.

EASY PEASY TOO

• There are lots of extras you can add. Try
capers, anchovies, cubes of your favourite
cheese, nuts or chopped apple.
• Make the same salad using rice instead
of pasta. Cook the rice as explained on
page 49, then add the vegetables of your
choice and the dressing.
• Try using just mayonnaise, lemon juice
and black pepper as an alternative dressing
for the pasta salad.

Cows Cows Salad

This salad is nothing to do with cows – it is just our way of saying 'cous cous'!

You will need:

150g of instant cous cous
250ml of boiling water from the kettle
the juice of half a lemon
3 tablespoons of olive oil
2 tomatoes
a chunk of cucumber
a quarter each of red and yellow peppers,
    washed and chopped into small pieces
1 spring onion, sliced finely
lots of chopped herbs: mint, parsley or
    coriander
some salt and pepper

a large bowl
a heat-proof measuring jug
a fork
a sharp knife and a chopping board
cling film

1. Put the cous cous in the bowl and the boiling water (boil the water in a kettle, then measure it in the jug). Stir it around with the fork until it soaks up all the water – this will take a few minutes.
2. Add the lemon juice and the olive oil and fluff it up with the fork again.
3. Add the chopped vegetables and herbs and some salt and pepper.
4. Taste it and add more salt and pepper or lemon juice if you want.
5. Cover it with cling film and put it in the fridge for a while before serving. This will improve the flavour.

Soups

Before you begin:

- Easy Peasy means being prepared. Get everything ready before you start cooking.

- Each recipe serves 4 people, unless we tell you otherwise.

- If the recipe tells you to do something you don't understand, look back at the sections on 'Easy Peasy Pots and Pans' (page 18) and 'How To Do Everything Brilliantly' (page 12).

- Remember to take care when using sharp knives and always use oven gloves when taking dishes in and out of the oven.

- When you have finished cooking, always remember to turn off the oven, cooker or grill.

Tomato Soupy

You will need:

1 large onion
a blob of butter
a tin of plum tomatoes (about 425g)
cold water
a handful of fresh basil or mint
1 teaspoon of sugar
salt
some cream

a sharp knife
a chopping board
a medium sized saucepan with a lid
a wooden spoon
a liquidiser
teaspoons

1. Peel the onion and slice it as thinly as you can.
2. Melt the butter in the saucepan over a low heat.
3. Add the onions, stir them with the wooden spoon and let them cook very slowly until they're soft and clear. This will take about 15 minutes.
4. Add the tomatoes and 2 can-fulls of cold water.
5. Wash the herbs, tear them up and put them into the saucepan. Add the sugar.
6. On a high heat bring the soup to the boil, put the lid on, turn the heat down very low and cook gently for about 30 minutes.

7. Let it cool a little and then carefully pour it into a liquidiser. Put the lid on and whizz the soup until it's smooth. Make sure you don't splash yourself.
8. Pour it back into the saucepan, add about a teaspoon of salt and warm it through. Taste it and add more water if it's too thick and more salt if you want it.

It's even more gorgeous if you serve it with a blob of fresh cream and some more chopped fresh herbs.

EASY PEASY TOO
TOMATO AND RICE SOUP

Add 2 tablespoons of rice to the soup, with an extra couple of cups of cold water after you've liquidised it. Cook it gently for another 20 minutes.

Cowboy Soup

You will need:

a tin of red kidney beans (about 425g)
2 medium sized red peppers, washed,
    trimmed and cut into chunks
a large knob of butter
2 large onions, peeled and chopped
500g of lean minced beef
salt and black pepper
1 tin of chopped tomatoes (about 425g)
900ml of hot water from the kettle

a sieve
a sharp knife
a chopping board
a medium sized saucepan with a lid
a wooden spoon
a measuring jug
a liquidiser or hand-held blender

1. Drain the kidney beans into the sieve. Rinse them with cold water.
2. Cut the peppers in half lengthways, wash out the little white seeds and cut off the stalk at the top. Chop the pepper into chunks.
3. Melt the butter in the saucepan on a low heat and add the onions. Cook them for about 10 minutes until they're soft. Stir them occasionally with the wooden spoon.
4. Turn the heat up high and add the minced beef. Keep turning it over with the spoon until it turns brown all over. Add a teaspoon of salt and about 8 grindings of black pepper.

5. Now add the tomatoes, beans, peppers and hot water.
6. When it starts to boil, turn the heat right down so that it just bubbles gently.
7. Give it a stir, put the lid on and cook it for about 1½ hours.
8. Taste it to check the flavour and add more salt if you want.
9. When it's cooled down a bit, carefully pour it into the liquidiser, or use a blender, and blend it until it's fairly smooth with just a few lumps.

This makes quite a big pot of soup so you may want to freeze some of it. Make sure it's completely cold before it goes into the freezer in a sealed container. Label it with the date it was frozen. It will last for up to three months. Defrost it completely before heating it through again.

Pot and Pasta Soup

You will need:

2 tablespoons of olive oil
1 peeled clove of garlic
1 small onion, peeled and chopped
3 potatoes, peeled and chopped into
    cubes
500g carton or bottle of tomato passata
    (or a 425g tin of chopped tomatoes,
    sieved)
the empty carton or bottle filled twice with
    cold water
salt
3 handfuls of chunky pasta
grated Parmesan cheese

a sharp knife and a chopping board
a vegetable peeler
a wooden spoon
a medium sized saucepan with a lid

1. Put the saucepan on the cooker on a low heat and add the oil.
2. Add the onion and garlic and cook very slowly, stirring from time to time with the wooden spoon.
3. Add the tomatoes, potatoes and the water.
4. Turn up the heat until the soup starts to boil, then lower it.
5. Let the soup cook very slowly with the lid on for about 1 hour, stirring it now and then to stop it sticking.
6. When the potatoes are soft, add the pasta and a little more water. Stir it and cook for another 10 minutes.
7. Taste it and add more salt if you want.
8. Serve with grated Parmesan on top.

EASY PEASY TOO

• You can use a handful of rice instead of pasta.

Fowl Soup

You will need:

2 sticks of celery
1 small onion, peeled
1 carrot, peeled
about 500g of chicken portions (legs
    and thighs)
1 litre of cold water
a big bunch of fresh, washed parsley
salt
2 handfuls of thin noodles
grated Parmesan cheese

a vegetable peeler
a chopping board
2 sharp knives
a meat chopping board
a medium sized saucepan with a lid
a measuring jug
a small tea-strainer sized sieve
a small bowl
a wooden spoon
a large strainer or sieve with a large bowl

1. Wash all the vegetables and cut them into big pieces.
2. Wash the chicken and cut off any loose bits of fat or skin.
3. Put the chicken into the saucepan with the water, turn the heat up high and bring it to the boil.
4. Lower the heat so the soup just bubbles gently and using the small sieve, skim any scum off the top. Keep doing this until the water is clear.

5. Add all the vegetables, the parsley and a teaspoon of salt.
6. Put the lid on and let the soup cook for about 1½ hours.
7. Taste it and add some more salt if you want. Remember the soup will be very hot.
8. Leave the soup to cool.
9. When it has cooled down, the last bits of fat will lie on the surface. Lift them off with a spoon and pour the soup through the big strainer and into the larger bowl. Keep the chicken pieces and vegetables separately but throw out everything else.
10. When you're ready to eat, heat the soup on the cooker and add the noodles. Let this cook through for another 10 minutes.
11. Take the chicken off the bones and add that too. Taste it and some salt if you want it.
12. Lastly, add a handful of freshly chopped parsley and serve with some grated Parmesan cheese.

EASY PEASY TOO

• Once you've strained the soup it can be used as chicken stock to make lots of other soups.
• Try mixing together an egg and a dessert-spoon of Parmesan cheese and whisking it in to the soup. Let it cook for another 5 minutes.

Bits and Bobs Soup

You will need:

2 tablespoons of olive oil
1 clove of garlic, peeled and chopped
2 slices of smoked bacon
1 small onion, peeled and finely chopped
2 carrots, finely chopped
2 sticks of celery, finely chopped
1 tin of chopped tomatoes (about 425g)
500ml of hot water from the kettle
2 handfuls of small, chunky pasta
salt
2 tablespoons of grated Parmesan cheese
some fresh basil leaves

a medium saucepan with a lid
a sharp knife
scissors
a vegetable peeler
a chopping board
a wooden spoon

1. Put the olive oil into the saucepan and warm it over a low heat.
2. Add the garlic and let it cook for a few minutes to flavour the oil.
3. Chop the bacon into small bits with the scissors and add it to the saucepan. Stir it all around with the wooden spoon and let it cook for about 5 minutes.
4. Now add all the vegetables, except the tomatoes, and stir them around. Let them cook slowly for 10-15 minutes to soften them.

5. Lastly, add the tomatoes and the water. Heat the soup until it's gently bubbling and put the lid on. Leave it for 1 hour.
6. Add the pasta and a bit more water if it needs it and cook for another 10-12 minutes.
7. Taste it and add some salt and the fresh basil leaves.
8. Serve it with the Parmesan cheese sprinkled on top.

EASY PEASY TOO

• Add half a tin of drained cannellini beans when you add the pasta.

See in the Dark Soup

You will need:

a big blob of butter
1 medium onion, peeled and sliced
6 carrots, peeled and roughly chopped
2 sticks of celery, washed and chopped
1 medium potato, peeled and chopped
1 litre of boiling water from the kettle
salt
some freshly washed and chopped herbs:
    parsley, coriander or mint.
some cream

a medium sized saucepan with a lid
a sharp knife
a wooden spoon
a vegetable peeler
a chopping board
a measuring jug
a teaspoon
a liquidiser or hand-held blender

1. Melt the butter in the saucepan on a medium heat.
2. Add the onions and stir them around with the wooden spoon. Turn the heat right down and let them soften for about 10 minutes.
3. Add the vegetables, stirring them around as well, and let them cook for another 10 minutes.
4. Turn up the heat and carefully add the boiling water. Bring the soup to a gentle simmer and cook for 30 minutes with the lid on.
5. Taste it and add about a half a teaspoon of salt.
6. Turn the heat off and let the soup cool. Pour it into the liquidiser, or use the blender, and blend until it's as smooth as you like. Be careful not to splash yourself.
7. When you're ready to eat, warm the soup up on the cooker, taste it and add more water if it's too thick. Serve it with a blob of fresh cream and the fresh herbs.

EASY PEASY TOO

• Try adding a small chunk of finely sliced fresh ginger and a teaspoon of ground coriander when you first put the butter into the saucepan. Then serve the soup with some chopped, fresh coriander on top.

Oriental Soup

You will need:

1 litre of chicken stock (a chicken stock
   cube dissolved in boiling water is fine,
   or use the soup recipe on page 64)
a tin of sweetcorn (about 225g)
100g of cooked chicken, shredded
1 dessertspoon of soya sauce
1 teaspoon of fresh ginger, peeled and
   chopped
1 teaspoon of sugar
2 spring onions, finely chopped
3 teaspoons of cornflour
3 tablespoons of cold water
salt
1 egg white
1 teaspoon of sesame oil
1 tablespoon of fresh, chopped coriander

a measuring jug
a medium sized saucepan
a sieve
a vegetable peeler
a chopping board
a sharp knife
2 cups
teaspoons, tablespoons and a fork

1. Put the stock into the saucepan on
a low heat and bring it to a gentle boil.
2. Drain the sweetcorn into the sieve and
rinse it with cold water. Add it to the stock.
3. Add the chicken, soya sauce, ginger,
sugar and spring onions. Let it bubble
gently for a few minutes.

4. Mix the cornflour with the cold water in
the cup to make a smooth liquid.
5. Start to stir the soup with the fork and
gradually pour in the cornflour to thicken it.
6. Taste the soup and add some salt if it
needs it.
7. In another cup, mix the egg white with the
fork and pour that into the soup, whisking all
the time to make ribbons.
8. Add a final dash of flavour with the
sesame oil and chopped coriander.

EASY PEASY TOO

• Instead of the shredded chicken, you can
add chopped crab sticks or prawns.
• You can also add some sliced mushrooms
and cook them in the soup until they're
tender.

CORIANDER SOUP

1 litre of chicken stock
a large bunch of fresh coriander, washed
   and chopped
a small piece of fresh ginger, peeled and
   finely chopped
2 spring onions, washed, trimmed and sliced
a squeeze of lemon juice
2 handfuls of egg noodles

Simply add all these ingredients to the
chicken stock and cook them together for
10 minutes until the noodles are soft.

Fruit Soup

You will need:

half a sweet melon
10 strawberries
10 raspberries
half a banana
the juice of an orange or a cup of fresh
    orange juice
some sugar
some cream

a sharp knife
a chopping board
a liquidiser or hand-held blender
a serving bowl
a juice squeezer
a dessertspoon

1. Remove the seeds from the melon and scoop out the flesh with the spoon. Put half of it into the liquidiser and the other half into the serving bowl.
2. Wash the strawberries and cut off their stalks. Chop them into quarters and put half into the liquidiser and half into the serving bowl.
3. Put half the raspberries into the serving bowl and half into the liquidiser.
4. Peel the banana and slice it thinly. Put it all into the serving bowl.
5. Cut the orange in half, put it on the juice squeezer and twist so the juice comes out. Put the juice into the liquidiser.
6. Put the lid on and whizz everything. Pour over the fruit in the serving bowl.
7. Taste it and add some sugar if you'd like it sweeter.
8. Serve the soup with a swirl of fresh cream.

EASY PEASY TOO

• You can serve this soup as a starter if you whizz all the fruit in the liquidiser and serve it chilled with some freshly chopped mint instead of the cream.

I'm Starving

Before you begin:

- Easy Peasy means being prepared. Get everything ready before you start cooking.

- Each recipe serves 4 people, unless we tell you otherwise.

- If the recipe tells you to do something you don't understand, look back at the sections on 'Easy Peasy Pots and Pans' (page 18) and 'How To Do Everything Brilliantly' (page 12).

- Remember to take care when using sharp knives and always use oven gloves when taking dishes in and out of the oven.

- When you have finished cooking, always remember to turn off the oven, cooker or grill.

Jump in your Mouth

Ask an adult to help the first time you cook this recipe.

You will need:

8 small medallions of pork or turkey
salt and pepper
some cheese slices
some slices of smoked ham
a blob of butter
3 tablespoons of olive oil

greaseproof paper
a chopping board
a rolling pin
a sharp knife
toothpicks or cocktail sticks
a large frying pan
a spatula
a fork

1. Place each medallion of pork between 2 sheets of greaseproof paper on the chopping board.
2. Bash each one flat three or four times with the rolling pin to help make it tender.
3. Peel away the greaseproof paper and sprinkle on some salt and pepper.
4. Put a slice of cheese to fit on each piece of pork. Then add a slice of ham on top.
5. Use a toothpick to pin it together, in through the ham, the cheese and the pork and back up again, just as if you were sewing something.
6. Melt the butter and the oil in the frying pan, on a medium heat, for a few minutes.
7. Add the bundles, pork side down and cook for about 5 minutes until they're well browned.
8. Now, using the spatula and fork, turn them over and cook for another couple of minutes. Don't forget to remove the toothpicks when you serve them!

EASY PEASY TOO

• Try adding more flavour to these parcels by putting a fresh sage leaf onto the pork either instead of the cheese or as well as.

Sticky Chicken

You will need:

3 tablespoons of sunflower oil
2 tablespoons of honey
2 tablespoons of soya sauce
1 tablespoon of mustard
a pinch of cayenne pepper
8 skinless chicken thighs or drumsticks.

a medium sized bowl
tablespoons
a teaspoon
a wooden spoon
clingfilm
a baking tray or ovenproof dish big
   enough to hold the chicken
oven gloves
tongs
a skewer

1. Turn on the oven to 200ºC/400ºF/ gas mark 6.
2. Mix all the ingredients, except the chicken, together in the bowl and stir.
3. Rub the chicken in the sauce and cover them with clingfilm. Leave them in the fridge for an hour to soak up the juices. This is called marinating.
4. Lay the chicken pieces in a single layer on the baking tray or in the dish and using your oven gloves, put them on the middle shelf of the oven and cook them for about 15 minutes.
5. Take them out of the oven, using your oven gloves, and put the dish or tray somewhere safe.
6. Turn the chicken pieces over with the tongs and pop them back into the oven for another 15 minutes.
7. Now take them out of the oven carefully, with the oven gloves, and check they're cooked by piercing the biggest piece of chicken with the skewer. The juice that runs out will be clear. If it's pink or red the chicken needs to be cooked for longer.

EASY PEASY TOO

• This recipe works just as well with pork spare ribs. Try these next time.

Sizzle Stir

You will need:

1 clove of garlic, peeled and sliced
a small piece fresh ginger, washed
    and thinly sliced
2 carrots
1 small onion
1 small red pepper
some broccoli
2 spring onions
2 tablespoons of vegetable oil
3 tablespoons of soya sauce
2 teaspoons of sesame oil

a vegetable peeler
a chopping board
a sharp knife
tablespoons
teaspoons
a very large frying pan or a wok
a wooden spoon
a warm serving plate

1. Wash all the vegetables and peel those
that need peeling. Cut them up into match-
stick sized pieces. This takes quite a long
time but it's good fun. Keep all the
different vegetables in separate bundles.
2. Check the list of ingredients and make
sure everything is chopped and laid out
ready to cook.
3. Heat the vegetable oil over a high heat
in the frying pan or wok.
4. Add the garlic and ginger and stir them
around with the wooden spoon. This
flavours the oil.

5. Now start to add the vegetables, choosing
the hardest ones first – carrots, onions,
peppers, broccoli and, lastly, spring onions.
Stir them around for a few minutes and add
the soya sauce and mix thoroughly.
6. As soon as the vegetables are cooked but
still crisp, tip them onto a warmed plate.
7. Sprinkle with the sesame oil and serve
right away.
8. Serve with *Easy Peasy rice* on Page 49.

EASY PEASY TOO

• You can use any combination of vegetables
you like when you stir fry. Ginger, garlic and
spring onions are almost always needed. But
try beansprouts, green beans, cauliflower,
mushrooms, leeks, anything in the fridge.
• You can add thin slices of chicken or beef.
Cut it in small slivers the same size as the
vegetables and let it sit in a bowl with a
couple of tablespoons of soya sauce for an
hour before cooking. This is called marinating.
It helps to give the meat or chicken flavour
and tenderness. When you're stir frying with
meat or chicken, add it to the frying pan or
wok after the ginger and garlic but before the
vegetables. Then cook it in the hot oil for a
few minutes before adding the rest of the
ingredients.

Grilled Chop Chop

You will need:

4 lamb chops
a clove of garlic, peeled and sliced into
    very thin slivers
some sprigs of fresh rosemary
olive oil
salt and pepper

a meat chopping board
a sharp knife
the grill pan
oven gloves
tongs

1. Put the grill on before you start as it needs to be hot.
2. Lay the chops on the chopping board and make 2 small, thin slits in each one with the sharp knife.
3. Push a sliver of garlic and a small sprig of rosemary into each slit.
4. Put the chops onto the grill pan, side by side and sprinkle each one with a little olive oil, salt and pepper.
5. Using your oven gloves, place them under the grill for 10 minutes.
6. Then, very carefully, pull the grill pan out and turn the chops over. Add another little sprinkling of olive oil, salt and pepper.
7. Grill them for another 5 minutes or so.
8. Serve the chops with the grilled garlic and rosemary.

Middle Finger

You will need:

about 6 tablespoons of flour
6 tablespoons of bread crumbs
1 egg
salt and pepper
2 fillets of white fish – haddock,
   lemon sole or cod (about 200g)
sunflower or vegetable oil
a small cube of dry bread

a tablespoon
3 large plates
a small bowl
a fork
a chopping board
a sharp knife
a frying pan
a fish slice
a serving plate
kitchen paper

1. Put the flour onto one plate and the bread crumbs onto another.
2. Break the egg into the bowl and season it with a little salt and pepper. Beat it with the fork.
3. Wash the fish in cold water and press the flesh with your fingers to check there are no bones. If there are, cut them out with the knife.
4. Cut the fish up into pieces about the length of your middle finger and two fingers thick.
5. Wash and dry your hands. Using your right hand only (left if you're left handed), dip the fish into the flour first, then the egg mixture and finally into the bread crumbs. Leave them on a plate.
6. Wash your hands again.
7. Heat enough oil to fill the frying pan half way up. Add a cube of bread and wait for it to start sizzling. The oil is now hot enough to add the fish fingers. Cook four or five at a time depending on the size of the frying pan.
8. Cook them until they are browning underneath, then use the fish slice to turn them over and cook the other side. When they're browned all over put them onto the serving plate which has been covered with a sheet of kitchen paper. This helps to drain off all the oil.
9. Keep the cooked fish in a warm place, such as the oven, until you've cooked them all.

EASY PEASY TOO
VEGGY FINGERS

Try cutting finger-sized slices of courgettes, peppers or aubergines. Dip them in the flour, egg and bread crumbs and fry them in exactly the same way. They take a little longer to cook and are particularly good with mayonnaise.
• You could also try onion rings. They also take a little longer to cook.

CHICKEN FINGERS

Exactly the same but using cooked chicken breast cut into fingers. These are lovely with *Easy Peasy Saucy Salsa* on page 82.

Cheesy Fish

You will need:

4 fillets of lemon sole
salt and pepper
4 tablespoons of double cream
2 tablespoons of grated cheese

a chopping board
a sharp knife
kitchen paper
an ovenproof dish
2 tablespoons
oven gloves

1. Put the grill on before you start to cook as it needs to be hot.
2. Press the fish with your fingers to make sure there are no bones. If there are, cut them out with the sharp knife.
3. Wash them under cold water and pat dry with kitchen paper.
4. Put the fish into the ovenproof dish and sprinkle with a little salt and pepper.
5. Cover each piece with a tablespoon of double cream and some of the grated cheese.
6. Using your oven gloves, put the dish under the grill and cook for about 10-15 minutes until the cheese melts and gets crisp.
7. Take the fish out of the grill, using the oven gloves and put it somewhere safe.
8. Check it's cooked by piercing it with the sharp knife. If it's cooked the knife will press through easily. If it doesn't, cook the fish for a bit longer.

Spicy Bites

You will need:

a tin of chickpeas or butter beans
   (about 425g)
1 small onion, peeled and chopped
1 small clove of garlic, peeled and chopped
1 teaspoon of ground cumin
1 teaspoon of ground coriander
a big handful of fresh, chopped coriander
   or parsley
half a teaspoon of baking powder
4 tablespoons of water
salt and pepper
plain flour
about 8 tablespoons of sunflower or
   vegetable oil

a sieve
a vegetable chopping board
a sharp knife
teaspoons, tablespoons and forks
a food processor
a bowl
clingfilm
2 plates
a frying pan
a spatula
a serving plate
kitchen paper

1. Drain the chickpeas or butter beans into the sieve and rinse them well under cold water.

2. Add all the ingredients, except the flour and the vegetable oil, to the food processor. Add some salt and pepper and whizz everything to make a paste. If you don't have a food processor, just chop everything as finely as possible and mash it with a fork.

3. Tip everything into the bowl, cover it and leave it for 30 minutes in the fridge.

4. Tip some flour onto a plate and have a second, empty plate ready.

5. The mixture is quite sticky. Wash your hands and then dust them with some flour. Shape the mixture into little balls. Flatten them down a little to make small rounds and coat each one in flour. Lay them on the plate.

6. Heat the vegetable oil in the frying pan and add a small piece of the mixture. When it starts to sizzle, lay half the spicy bites in the pan for about 3 minutes until they're brown and crisp on the bottom. You may have to lower the heat so they cook well but don't burn. Be careful as they can spit and splash.

7. Using the spatula, carefully turn them over and cook the other side. Drain them on the kitchen paper. These are gorgeous but delicate. Don't worry if they break up a bit.

CUCUMBER AND YOGHURT DIP

These spicy little bites are great with a cucumber and yoghurt dip. Peel and chop a chunk of cucumber and some fresh coriander. Mix it in a bowl with a tub of natural yoghurt. Add some ground coriander to flavour it and a little chilli powder if you like things to be spicy and hot. Be careful! Chilli powder and dried chilli sting if you put them near your lips or eyes. Always use a spoon when you're measuring it or, in the case of dried chilli, wash your hands very well after touching it. Ask an adult to help the first time you try this recipe.

Topped Tarts

You will need:

some plain flour
a pack of de-frosted, frozen puff pastry
   (about 125g)
butter for greasing
1 egg
2 large, sliced tomatoes
salt and pepper
fresh basil or finely chopped parsley
a pile of grated Cheddar cheese

a rolling pin
a vegetable chopping board
a sharp knife
a pastry cutter (about 6cm round)
a greased baking sheet
a cup
a fork
a small bowl
a pastry brush
oven gloves

1. Turn on the oven to 200ºC/400ºF/
gas mark 6.
2. Sprinkle a clean, dry work surface with
a little flour. Put some on the rolling pin
as well and roll out the pastry to about
the thickness of a wooden spoon.
3. Using the pastry cutter, cut out as many
rounds as you can and put them on the
greased baking sheet.

4. Break the egg into a cup and beat it with
a fork.
5. Paint the pastry with a little beaten egg.
6. Put a slice of tomato onto each pastry ring
and sprinkle on some salt, pepper and the
chopped herbs.
7. Top each tomato with plenty of grated
cheese.
8. Using your oven gloves, pop the baking
sheet into the oven for about 10 minutes
until the pastry is golden brown and the
cheese melted.
9. Carefully remove the tray from the oven
with your oven gloves. Let the tarts cool a bit
before eating them as they will be very hot.

EASY PEASY TOO

• Try adding smoked ham or thin slices of
mushroom under the cheese.
• Try some pesto on the tomatoes before
you put them into the oven.
• Make a sweet version by topping the pastry
with some raspberry jam and half a fresh
plum. Sprinkle it with some soft brown sugar
and cinnamon to make a sweet, crunchy
topping. Good with whipped cream.
• Easy Peasy Jam Roly Poly: if you've got any
left-over pastry, gather it all into a ball and
roll it out into a flat sheet. Spread it with jam
and sprinkle on some soft brown sugar. Roll
up the pastry and cut it into finger-sized
pieces. Bake them in the oven on a greased
baking tray for about 8-10 minutes.

Saucy Salsa

You will need:

a big chunk of cucumber
4 ripe tomatoes
1 spring onion
a handful of fresh mint leaves and some
   fresh parsley, washed and chopped
1 tablespoon of olive oil
1 teaspoon of lemon juice
a little sugar
salt

a sharp knife
a chopping board
a vegetable peeler
a medium-sized bowl
a wooden spoon
teaspoons

1. Peel the cucumber and chop it into tiny
cubes. Put it into the bowl.
2. Wash the tomatoes and cut them into
quarters. Remove the seeds and chop the
tomato into tiny pieces. Put them in the
bowl too.
3. Wash and trim the spring onion, slice
it finely and add to the bowl.
4. Now add the herbs, oil, lemon juice,
sugar and a little salt. Mix it all together
and taste it. Add more salt or sugar if you
think it needs it.
5. Cover the saucy salsa and leave it in
the fridge for an hour before eating. This
is lovely as a dip, with fish or meat or
simply spread on bread.

EASY PEASY TOO
SWEET FRUITY SALSA

Chop up a mango and a banana into tiny
cubes. Add a teaspoon of sultanas, a
tablespoon of lime juice, a dessertspoon
of demerara sugar and a handful of chopped
mint. Mix everything and taste it. Cover and
leave it in the fridge for an hour.

AVOCADO AND TOMATO
SPICY SALSA

Chop up a ripe avocado and 2 tomatoes into
tiny cubes. Mix them in a bowl with a quarter
of a red onion, very finely chopped. Flavour
with a handful of chopped coriander leaves
and add a quarter of a teaspoon of curry
powder. Mix in 2 tablespoons of natural
yoghurt. Season with salt and a teaspoon
of lemon juice.

Chicken Burglars

You will need:

225 g chicken breast
1 medium onion
125 g breadcrumbs
1 handful chopped fresh parsley
large blob of tomato ketchup (if you fancy it)
salt and pepper
about 4 tablespoons of vegetable oil,
   for frying

chopping board
sharp knife
food processor (optional)
medium-sized bowl
a fork
scales
frying pan
spatula
kitchen paper
serving plate

1. Chop the chicken up very finely on the chopping board using the sharp knife, or in the food processor. Chop the onion very finely in the same way.

2. Put the chopped chicken and onion, the breadcrumbs, the parsley and the tomato ketchup (if using) in the bowl and mix them well together with the fork.

3. Add plenty of salt and pepper.

4. Wash your hands well. Take a handful of the mixture and mould it into a burger shape, about 1.5 cm thick. Use up nearly all the mixture to make burgers in this way, but keep a tiny bit for stage 6. (You should be able to make 8 burgers, that's 2 each.)

5. Heat the vegetable oil in the frying pan.

6. Add a tiny bit of the mixture and when it starts to sizzle, carefully add 4 of the chicken burgers. Cook them for about 5 minutes on each side, being careful when you turn them over (using the spatula) in case the oil splashes. If they're sizzling too much, turn the heat down.

7. When the burgers are cooked on both sides, take them out of the frying pan using the spatula and leave them to drain on the plate with the kitchen paper on it.

8. Cook the other 4 burgers the same way.

EASY PEASY TOO

These chicken burgers are gorgeous in a bread roll with some Saucy Salsa (see page 82, opposite), or even better with chips and loads of tomato ketchup.

bread

Before you begin:

- Easy Peasy means being prepared. Get everything ready before you start cooking.

- Each recipe serves 4 people, unless we tell you otherwise.

- If the recipe tells you to do something you don't understand, look back at the sections on 'Easy Peasy Pots and Pans' (page 18) and 'How To Do Everything Brilliantly' (page 12).

- Remember to take care when using sharp knives and always use oven gloves when taking dishes in and out of the oven.

- Easy Peasy baking means being **very** accurate when you weigh the ingredients.

- When you have finished cooking, always remember to turn off the oven, cooker or grill.

Pru's Loaf

You will need:

plenty of butter
300g of strong white bread flour
150g of wholemeal or granary flour
1 teaspoon of salt
1 teaspoon of soft brown sugar
1 sachet of easy blend instant dried yeast
about 325ml of warm water (about the
    temperature of your bath!)

*a warm, draught-free place to let the
    dough rise in*
kitchen paper
a 900g (2lb) loaf tin
weighing scales
a large mixing bowl
a teaspoon
a wooden spoon
a measuring jug
a clean tea towel
oven gloves
a wire cooling rack

1. Using the kitchen paper and lots of butter, grease the loaf tin really well, remembering the corners and the rim.
2. Put all the flour, salt, sugar and yeast into the bowl and mix it together.
3. Now, using the wrong end of the wooden spoon to stir, add the warm water and mix everything round to form a dough. As it thickens, it will make a ball that will leave the sides the bowl and stick to the handle of the spoon. You need to mix as hard and as fast as you can, using a lot of muscle.

4. If the dough is a bit sloppy, add a little more flour. If it's too solid or dry, add a little more warm water. The dough should be quite soft and a little sticky.
5. Tip the whole lot into the loaf tin and gently press it down and into the corners.
6. Cover the tin with a clean tea towel and leave it in a warm, draught-free place for about an hour or until it has doubled in size.
7. Turn on the oven to 190°C/360°F/gas mark 4.
8. When the dough has doubled in size, remove the towel and, using your oven gloves, pop the tin into the oven and cook it for about 30 minutes until it is brown.
9. Carefully take it out of the oven and using your oven gloves, tip it out onto a wire cooling rack.
10. To check whether it's cooked, tap its bottom with your knuckles and listen for a hollow sound. If you don't hear it, put the bread back into the tin and into the oven for another 10 minutes.

EASY PEASY TOO

You can change the flavour of the loaf by adding seeds, nuts or dried fruits to the flour before you add the water.
• Try a teaspoon of poppy seeds or sunflower seeds.
• Try a small handful of raisins, sultanas or walnuts.

Drizzle Toast

You will need:

4 slices of thick country-style white bread
   or ciabatta bread
2 cloves of garlic, peeled and cut in half
4 tablespoons of olive oil
a little salt

a bread board
a sharp knife
a toaster or grill pan
a tablespoon
serving plate

1. Toast the bread or grill it if it's too thick for the toaster.
2. While the bread is warm, rub half a clove of garlic over each slice until the garlic has almost melted.
3. Drizzle each slice with a tablespoon of olive oil and a little sprinkling of salt.
4. Eat it while it's still warm.

EASY PEASY TOO

You can add any toppings you like to this garlicky Italian toast.
• Try sliced tomatoes with fresh basil.
• Try some sliced tomatoes and Mozzarella cheese. Melt under the grill for a few minutes.
• Try some salami with some stoned olives, piled onto salad leaves.

Cubes

You will need:

about 6 tablespoons of olive oil
3 slices of dry bread

a medium sized bowl
a sharp knife
a chopping board
a slotted spoon
a baking tray
oven gloves
a serving plate
kitchen paper

1. Turn on the oven to 200°C/400°F/ gas mark 6.
2. Put the oil into the bowl.
3. Cut the bread into small cubes and add them to the bowl.
4. Mix them around until they're well oiled.
5. Using the slotted spoon, to drain off excess oil, put the cubes onto the baking tray.
6. Using your oven gloves, pop them into the oven for about 5-7 minutes until they're brown and crisp. Check them half way through to make sure they're not burning.
7. Using oven gloves, take them out of the oven and drain them on kitchen paper.
8. They can be served hot in soups or warm in salads.

EASY PEASY TOO

• To make flavoured soup cubes, try adding pesto, dried herbs, chopped garlic or rock salt to the oil.

Crumbs

You will need:

dry bread

a liquidiser or food processor

1. Break the bread into chunks and put it into the liquidiser or food processor. (Put the lid on!)
2. Now whizz it until you've got bread crumbs. You can keep them in a sealed container for about 4 weeks.

Leggy Bread

You will need:

2 eggs
salt
2 slices of white or brown bread, cut
  in half
a large blob of butter
sugar

*a shallow dish like a soup plate, big
  enough to hold the bread*
a fork
a knife
a frying pan
a spatula
a plate

1. Crack the eggs into the dish. Add some salt and whisk them with the fork.
2. Add the bread to the mixture and turn it over so it gets good and soggy.
3. Heat the butter in the frying pan, on a medium heat, until it starts to foam.
4. Using the spatula, put the leggy bread into the hot butter, one layer at a time. Cook for a few minutes until it's brown on the bottom. Turn it over and cook the other side.
5. Put the cooked bread onto the plate and sprinkle it with some sugar.

EASY PEASY TOO CHEESY BREAD

Add a tablespoon of grated Cheddar cheese to the egg mixture to make cheese-flavoured leggy bread. You will not need to add any sugar.

FRUIT BREAD

This is delicious if you make it with slices of fruit-bread and sprinkle it with soft brown sugar and ground cinnamon.

pizza Dough

If you have a food processor with a dough hook you can do steps 1-3 in 3 or 4 minutes.

For the pizza base you will need:

350g of strong white plain flour
1 sachet of instant, easy-blend dried yeast
a teaspoon of salt
210ml of warm water (about the same
   temperature as your bath!)
olive oil

*a warm, draught-free place to let the
  dough rise in
a clean work surface
weighing scales
a sieve
a large mixing bowl
a wooden spoon
a measuring jug
a teaspoon
cling film
2 baking trays*

1. Sieve the flour into the bowl and add the yeast and salt. Mix them together with the wooden spoon.
2. Add the warm water and 1½ tablespoons of olive oil. Mix everything together until it forms a ball of dough, leaving the sides of the bowl clean.
3. Put a little extra flour on your hands and put the dough onto a clean work surface. Now, pressing and pushing with your hands, knead it until it's smooth and elastic. This will take about 10 minutes.
4. Grease the bowl with a little olive oil and put the dough back in. Cover it with clingfilm and leave it somewhere warm for about 1½ hours, until it has doubled in size.
5. Now make the pizza sauce, on the next page.

Pizza Sauce

For the sauce you will need:

a tin of chopped tomatoes (about 425g)
salt
1 clove of garlic, peeled and sliced
olive oil
1 teaspoon of dried oregano or some
    fresh basil leaves

a bowl
a sharp knife
a chopping board
a tablespoon
a teaspoon
clingfilm

1. Tip the tomatoes into the bowl.
2. Add the salt, garlic, 3 tablespoons of
olive oil and the herbs.
3. Mix it together, cover with clingfilm and
leave to stand while the dough is rising.
4. We've made the dough. We've made
the sauce. Now let's put it all together.
Turn over the page.

pizza

You will need:

olive oil
pizza dough – see page 92
pizza topping – see page 93
other extra toppings – see step 7
flour

a clean work surface
2 large baking sheets
kitchen paper
tablespoons
oven gloves

1. Turn on the oven to 230°C/450°F/ gas mark 8.

2. Using the kitchen paper, grease the baking trays with oil, remembering to cover all the corners.

3. Punch the dough in the bowl with your fists to knock out some of the air. Then tip it onto the clean work surface that has been dusted with flour and knead it again for about 2-3 minutes.

4. Split the dough in half and put a ball onto each baking tray.

5. Using your fingertips and the palms of your hands, press the dough out into a pizza shape as thick or as thin as you like.

6. Spread a couple of tablespoons of the tomato sauce onto each pizza base. Don't let it run over the edge.

7. Now you can add any topping you fancy. How about grated or sliced Mozzarella cheese, spicy sausage, fresh tomatoes, olives, anchovies or capers? Or smoked ham, mushrooms and pineapple?

8. Once you've decided on your topping, sprinkle a little more olive oil over the top and, using your oven gloves, pop the pizza into the oven for about 15 minutes until it's crisp and golden.

Rise Again

You will need:

pizza dough – see page 88
more olive oil
rosemary or sage leaves
sea salt

2 baking trays
kitchen paper

1. Turn on the oven to 230ºC/450ºF/
gas mark 8.
2. Divide the dough into four and, using your
hands, press them out into circles or ovals
on the baking trays.
3. Dribble some olive oil over the top and
press some rosemary or sage leaves and
some coarse sea salt into the dough.
4. Leave it for about 15-20 minutes to let it
rise a little again.
5. Using your oven gloves, pop them into the
oven for about 12 minutes until they're crisp
and golden underneath.

Toastie

For 1 person

You will need:

lots of Cheddar cheese (ready grated
  is easiest)
2 slices of white or wholemeal bread
butter

a sharp knife
a chopping board
a grill pan
a serving plate
a knife for buttering
oven gloves

1. Turn the grill on high.
2. If you don't have grated cheese, slice
the cheddar into very thin slices.
3. Put the bread on the grill pan and grill
one side of it.
4. Using your oven gloves, carefully take
the grill pan out and put the toast on the
chopping board. Butter the un-toasted side.
5. Pile the grated cheese on the toast and
push it down with your hands.
6. Using your oven gloves, carefully put the
toast back under the grill until the cheese
has melted and gone a little brown.

EASY PEASY TOO

• Add some Worcestershire sauce to the
toast before you add the cheese. This gives
it a lovely spicy taste.
• Try some smoked ham and sliced tomatoes
before adding the cheese. Remember to salt
and pepper the tomatoes.

Knock-out Bread

For 2 people

You will need:

lots and lots of soft butter
4 cloves of peeled garlic
1 long French baguette

a small bowl
a garlic crusher
a fork
a sharp knife
a chopping board
a knife for buttering
tin foil
oven gloves

1. Turn on the oven to 200ºC/400ºF/ gas mark 6.
2. Put the butter into the bowl. Put the garlic into the garlic crusher, hold it over the bowl and squeeze the garlic into the butter. Mix well with the fork to make the garlic butter.
3. Lay the baguette on the chopping board and using the sharp knife, cut the bread down into slices but only half-way so they remain attached to the loaf but can be prised apart.
4. Now press lots of the garlic butter into each slice, pushing them together again.
5. Use the remaining butter to spread over the top and the sides of the baguette.

6. Wrap the whole loaf loosely in tin foil, folding it over at the ends to seal the parcel well.
7. Using your oven gloves, pop it into the oven for 30 minutes.
8. When you open the parcel be careful of the steam. Chop the slices all the way through to separate them.

EASY PEASY TOO HERBY GARLIC BREAD

Add a handful of chopped herbs to the garlic butter. Try parsley, rosemary or sage.

PIZZA BREAD

Slice 2 tomatoes and some Mozzarella cheese. Make the Easy Peasy Knock-out Bread and push a slice of tomato and mozzarella between each slice. You can also add some fresh chopped basil. Cook it in exactly the same way. Be careful to let it cool a little before eating because the cheese can be very hot.

Mary Rose

You will need:

125g pack of frozen prawns, defrosted
2 tablespoons of mayonnaise
2 tablespoons of thick double cream
1 tablespoon of tomato ketchup
1 teaspoon of tomato purée
1 teaspoon of Worcestershire sauce
1 teaspoon of Tabasco sauce (you don't
   have to use this, but it makes the sauce
   spicy)
1 teaspoon of lemon juice
1 teaspoon of very, very finely chopped
   onion

a sieve
a medium sized bowl
tablespoons, dessertspoons, teaspoons
   and a fork
a sharp knife
a chopping board

1. When the prawns have defrosted, put them in the sieve and rinse them with plenty of cold water. This takes away any stale water they have around them.
2. Allow them to drain.
3. Put everything except the prawns into the bowl and mix together. Taste it and add a little more ketchup if you want it sweeter, a little more lemon juice if you want it sharper and if you want it spicier, add a little more Tabasco.
4. Add the drained prawns and gently mix it all together.

EASY PEASY TOO

• You can eat this by itself or packed into a crunchy baguette or piled onto a slice of bread, with a layer of cucumber or lettuce on the bottom, to make a topless sandwich.

Topless Sandwiches

For 1 person

You will need:

2 slices of rye bread or any bread with
   the crusts cut off
some soft butter
2 slices of cheese
2 slices of smoked ham
2 slices of cucumber
2 slices of tomato
2 tablespoons of mayonnaise
some salt and pepper

a sharp knife
a chopping board
a tablespoon
a knife for buttering
a plate

1. Butter each slice of bread lightly.
2. Pile on the cheese, ham, cucumber and tomato with a little salt and pepper, using a little blob of mayonnaise between the layers to stick it all together.
3. Add a blob of mayonnaise on the top.
4. Serve it on the plate with a knife and fork.

EASY PEASY TOO

You can put anything you fancy on a topless sandwich. You usually need mayonnaise or chutney to moisten the fillings and stick them together.
• Try salami, tuna, sliced eggs or pastrami.
• Try gherkins, cream cheese and pineapple.

Get Stuffed

You will need:

1 large red pepper
2 courgettes
200g of bread crumbs
2 tablespoons of fresh, finely chopped
    parsley
1 clove of garlic, peeled and chopped
olive oil
salt and pepper

a sharp knife
a chopping board
a medium sized bowl
2 tablespoons
a baking tray
kitchen paper
tin foil
oven gloves

1. Turn on the oven to 190ºC/375ºF/ gas mark 5.

2. Wash the pepper, chop off the stalk and cut it in half lengthways. Scrape out all the seeds.

3. Wash the courgettes, cut them in half lengthways, scooping out a little of the middle. Then chop them up into small cubes. Put them in the bowl.

4. Put all the other ingredients into the bowl, with 4 tablespoons of olive oil and mix together. Add some salt and pepper and taste the stuffing to make sure there's enough salt. Add a little more oil if the mixture is dry.

5. Using kitchen paper, grease the baking tray.

6. Now stuff each of the pepper halves with plenty of the mixture, pressing it down well with the back of the spoon.

7. Lay each one on the baking tray and sprinkle them with a little more olive oil. Cover the tray with tin foil and bake in the oven for about 35-40 minutes. Let them cool a bit before you eat them.

EASY PEASY TOO

• Add some grated cheese or chopped tomatoes to the stuffing.
• If you like stronger flavours, add some chopped anchovies and capers.

Sweet Teeth

Before you begin:

- Easy Peasy means being prepared. Get everything ready before you start cooking.

- Each recipe serves 4 people, unless we tell you otherwise.

- If the recipe tells you to do something you don't understand, look back at the sections on 'Easy Peasy Pots and Pans' (page 18) and 'How To Do Everything Brilliantly' (page 12).

- Remember to take care when using sharp knives and always use oven gloves when taking dishes in and out of the oven.

- Easy Peasy baking means being **very** accurate when you weigh the ingredients.

- When you have finished cooking, always remember to turn off the oven, cooker or grill.

whatever you like Muffins

You will need:

50g of butter
150g of self-raising flour
50g of caster sugar
half a teaspoon of baking powder
1 egg
110ml of milk
120g of 'whatever you like' – choose from
   the list at the bottom of the page

a small saucepan
weighing scales
a sieve
large and small mixing bowls
a teaspoon
a wooden spoon
a fork
a measuring jug
a baking tray with 12 individual muffin
   shapes, each containing a paper case
a spatula
oven gloves
a skewer

1. Turn on the oven to 200ºC/400ºC/ gas mark 6.
2. Put the butter in the saucepan and melt it over a low heat. Let it cool a little.
3. Sieve the flour into the large mixing bowl and add the sugar and the baking powder. Mix everything together with the wooden spoon.
4. Break the egg into the small bowl and whisk it with the fork.
5. Add the egg and the milk to saucepan of the melted butter. Mix well.

6. Pour it into the flour and mix everything quickly together with the fork. Don't mix for too long. The mixture should be floppy and a bit lumpy.
7. Now mix in the 'whatever you like' flavouring. Divide the mixture between the paper cases, using the spatula to scrape out the bowl.
8. Using your oven gloves, put the tray into the oven.
9. After about 20 minutes check the muffins. They should be risen and golden.
10. Using your oven gloves, take them out of the oven and push the skewer into the middle of one of them. If it comes out clean, they're cooked. If not, put them back into the oven for another 5 minutes. Leave to cool a little, but they're best eaten warm.

EASY PEASY TOO

Use this mixture to make different flavoured muffins by adding 120g of 'whatever you like' flavourings. Here are some suggestions:
• 100g of peeled and chopped apple with 20g of sultanas and half a teaspoon of ground cinnamon.
• 80g of peeled and chopped apple with 40g of fresh or frozen raspberries or strawberries. If using fresh fruits, keep aside about a tablespoon of the sugar from the recipe and toss the fruits in this separately, before adding them to the mixture.
• 2 peeled and chopped bananas with 10g of chopped pecan or walnuts.
• 120g of chocolate chips.

Sweet Salad

You will need:

1 ripe mango
1 small melon
1 large kiwi fruit
a small bunch of grapes
apple juice
sugar

a vegetable peeler
a chopping board
a sharp knife
a bowl
a dessertspoon
cling film

1. Peel the mango, the melon and the kiwi fruit. Remove the seeds and chop the fruit into small chunks. Put them into the bowl.
2. Wash the grapes, cut them in half and if they have pips, remove them. Put the grapes into the bowl.
3. Add some apple juice, and a little sugar and stir. Taste it adding more sugar if you want.
4. Cover the bowl with cling film and put it in the fridge until you're ready to eat it.

EASY PEASY TOO
SUMMER BERRY BOWL

This is made in the same way using 2 small bananas, a punnet of raspberries, a punnet of strawberries, 1 kiwi fruit, some orange juice and some sugar.

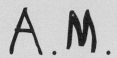

A.M.

This is called 'A.M.' because it's great for breakfast.

You will need:

4 apples
a punnet of strawberries
orange juice
some sugar
plain yoghurt

a vegetable peeler
a chopping board
a sharp knife
a saucepan with a lid
a spoon
a bowl

1. Peel the apples, cut into four and remove the core and pips. Chop the apple into small chunks and put them in the saucepan.
2. Wash the strawberries and cut off their stalks. Add them to the saucepan and pour in a small glass of orange juice.
3. Cook it all very gently on a low heat with the lid on until the apples become mushy when pressed with the back of the spoon.
4. Taste the mixture (remember it will be hot) and add a little sugar if you want it sweeter.
5. Let it cool a little and eat it by itself or with some plain yoghurt.

EASY PEASY TOO

• Try using a stick of cinnamon and some chopped no-soak dried apricots instead of the strawberries. Remember not to eat the cinnamon stick – take it out of the saucepan and throw it away after cooking.
• Try cooking a big pile of washed cherries, 3 peeled and chopped peaches or nectarines and a little apple juice the same way.

Banana Bread

You will need:

50g of soft butter and some extra for
   greasing the loaf tin
120g of castor sugar
half a teaspoon of salt
1 large egg
360g of self-raising flour
125ml of milk
3 bananas, peeled and chopped

a 450g (1lb) non-stick loaf tin
kitchen paper
a food processor or a mixing bowl with
   a wooden spoon
weighing scales
a chopping board
a sharp knife
a spatula
oven gloves
a skewer
a wire cooling rack

1. Turn on the oven to 175ºC/350ºF/
gas mark 4.
2. Grease the loaf tin with lots of butter,
making sure that you reach the corners.
3. Put all the ingredients, except the
bananas, into the food processor or bowl
and mix them.
4. Add the bananas and whisk everything
again.
5. Put the mixture into the loaf tin, scraping
everything out of the bowl with the spatula.
Using your oven gloves, put it onto the
middle shelf of the oven.
6. After about 45 minutes take it out of the
oven, using your oven gloves. It should be
golden brown and risen, with a slight crack
across the top.
7. Push the skewer into the middle and pull
it out. If it's cooked, the skewer will come
out clean. If not, pop it back into the oven
for another 10 minutes.
8. Let it cool in the tin for a few minutes
before tipping it out, using your oven gloves,
onto the wire cooling rack.

EASY PEASY TOO

• Try adding a tablespoon of chopped
walnuts or 2 tablespoons of chocolate chips.
• Try adding a teaspoon of mixed spice or
ground cinnamon.

Lassi

You will need:

2 ripe nectarines
8-10 raspberries
2-3 tablespoons of clear honey
1 large carton of full-fat yoghurt
some milk

a sharp knife
a chopping board
a liquidiser or a hand-held blender
a tablespoon
a mug of hot water
3 or 4 glasses

1. Peel the nectarines, cut out the stones and chop the fruit into chunks. Put them in the liquidiser or blender.
2. Add the raspberries.
3. Dip the tablespoon into a mug of hot water and spoon in 2 or 3 tablespoons of honey. (The hot water helps the honey slip easily into the blender.)
4. Add the yoghurt, put the lid on and whizz it until it's smooth. If it's too thick, add a little milk.
5. Pour into glasses and serve it chilled.

EASY PEASY TOO

• You can make Lassis with any soft fruits you like. Try mango and strawberries or kiwi fruit and mint.

wooden Leg

For 2 people

You will need:

2 oranges
10 strawberries or other soft berries
4 ice cubes

a sharp knife
a chopping board
a juice squeezer
a liquidiser or a hand-held blender
2 long glasses

1. Cut the oranges in half. Place each half on the juice squeezer and twist it around to squeeze out the juice. Pour the juice into the liquidiser.
2. Slice the stalks off the strawberries and add the strawberries to the liquidiser with the ice cubes.
3. Put the lid on and whizz.
4. Pour into glasses and serve it straight away before the ice melts.

Black Bananas

For 2 people

You will need:

2 large bananas in their skins
some demerara sugar
some cream
some ground cinnamon

a baking tray
oven gloves
2 serving plates
a sharp knife
spoons

1. Turn on the oven to 200°C/400°F/
gas mark 6.
2. Put the bananas, unpeeled, onto the
baking tray and using oven gloves, put them
into the oven until they're soft and black. It
usually takes about 25 minutes.
3. Using your oven gloves, pull the tray out
and slide the bananas onto the two serving
plates.
4. If they have not split open, cut them
straight down the middle.
5. Sprinkle them with a little sugar and pour
some cream on top. Add a little ground
cinnamon for extra flavour.
6. Eat them with a teaspoon, scooping out
the gooey flesh. Hide them from the monkeys!

Chocolate Mouse

You will need:

200g plain dark chocolate or 200g dark
    chocolate chips
300ml single cream
2 small free-range eggs
2 tablespoons of orange juice

a grater or sharp knife and chopping board
a plate
a measuring jug
a small saucepan
a liquidiser or a hand-held blender and its
    container
4 small glasses
cling film

1. Roughly grate the chocolate onto the plate or chop it into small pieces.
2. Put the cream in the saucepan and over a low heat, slowly bring it to the boil. Be careful it doesn't boil over.
3. Put the grated chocolate into the liquidiser or into the container and pour the hot cream over it. Whisk it for 30 seconds.
4. Break the eggs into the liquidiser or container, add the orange juice and whisk again.
5. Pour the mousse into the glasses, cover with clingfilm and chill in the fridge for a couple of hours.

THERE ARE RAW EGGS IN THIS RECIPE.
SO, IF YOU'RE VERY, VERY YOUNG
OR VERY, VERY OLD OR IF YOU'RE
PREGNANT IT'S NOT A BRILLIANT IDEA
TO EAT RAW EGGS.

How Not to poison yourself, your Family or your Friends

'Doctor! Doctor! Every bone in my body hurts!'
'Be grateful you're not a herring!'

Getting Ready

There's nothing worse than scrabbling around looking for an ingredient while something boils over on the cooker. The answer is get ready **before** you start cooking. Read the recipe all the way through, get everything out of the cupboards or fridge and arrange it all in order of use. Thereafter it's easy peasy.

washing your Hands

It's very important to cook with **clean** hands. Wash them (with soap!) before you start cooking and again at the end. You should also wash your hands after handling raw meat or fish, before you touch anything else.

Aprons

This is up to you but we always wear them so that we won't have to change our clothes every time we've whisked an egg!

Chopping Boards

It's best if you can have different coloured ones for different types of food, such as red for meat, blue for vegetables, green for fish and white for everything else. The reason why you should use different boards is so that you don't transfer any **nasty little bugs** from one to the other. However, most of us only have a couple of boards at home, so do your best. Just make sure they're very clean and that you don't use cooked foods on the same boards as raw foods.

work Surfaces

We know you'll think this is obvious but really do start cooking with **clean** work surfaces, 'specially if the cat has just walked over them! And by the way, they need to be clean when you've finished as well. We know – nag, nag, nag.

Knives

Sharp knives really are **sharp**. They need to be in order to work well, so be careful not to cut your finger off! Use a knife that's comfortable in your hand. Hold it and the food you're cutting firmly and keep your eyes open. Serrated knives are the ones with jagged blades. They're best used for things like slicing onions and tomatoes very finely.

water

If the recipe needs cold water then take it from the cold tap, letting it run a bit first. Hot water should always be taken from the kettle.

Frozen Foods

Be extra careful here. Unless you know that something can be cooked from frozen – like fish fingers – always **defrost** it completely before eating or cooking it. This is especially important with chicken and meat.

How to Avoid Blood, Sweat & Tears in the Kitchen

'Doctor! Doctor! I'm boiling!'
'Oh just simmer down!'

Sweat

Not the kind you get when the kitchen's too hot. It's the kind you'll be worked into if you don't clear up when you've finished – that's everything: saucepans, knives, spoons, tins, peelings, sticky stuff. Wipe over the cooker and the work surfaces. Always use clean cloths. Okay? No sweat!

Burns

There are endless ways to burn yourself in the kitchen. And there are some golden rules.
• Never leave the handle of a saucepan sticking out.
• Never leave a cooking spoon in the pan while something's cooking.
• Always use oven gloves to handle hot things.
• If you do burn yourself, turn off the heat and pour very **cold** water over the burn for at least ten minutes. It may feel like you're freezing to death but it'll take the sting out of the burn. Most kitchen burns are okay after that. Don't put a plaster over it. If your burn is serious, call an adult and get medical help.

heat

Heat is hot. Be careful. You'll be amazed at the heat that can come bursting out of the oven when you open the door. Even the **steam** from a saucepan can be very hot. Don't get too close to the gas burner when you switch on. Sometimes there's a delay between turning on the gas and it actually lighting. When that happens there's often a burst of **flame** that can come as a bit of a shock. It is the same principle with the oven. If you have pre-heated it, watch out when you open the door. Apart from the temperature, it'll steam up your glasses if you wear them. Also take care with food that's being cooked in a saucepan with a lid on. The heat and the steam will be horrible when you take the lid off. With the grill, be careful of your hands, arms, face and hair.

Cuts

They hurt a lot. Even little ones hurt and they give you a fright. One of the ways to avoid cutting yourself is to **concentrate** on what you're doing. If you do cut yourself, wash the cut under cold, running water, dry it and put a plaster on. Try not to cry – it affects the amount of salt in your dish! If the cut is a bad one, wrap it up tightly in a clean towel and call an adult.

Easy peasy up your Nose

Cooking is like painting. A dab of blue and a spot of yellow make green. A bag of flour, a few grammes of yeast and a jug-full of water make bread. Add to that some black treacle, garlic or cheese. Every new flavour or texture, like each new colour in a painting, adds another layer of sensation in your mouth. We can all make pictures in our imagination. We can all paint. And with a little experience we can all put together different foods to make dishes that look, smell and taste great. Just remember to use your nose, eyes, ears, mouth and feelings.

Close your eyes and shut your mouth. Breathe in deeply. What do you smell? Open your eyes. What can you see? Close your eyes and put a piece of chocolate into your mouth. What do you taste? Close your eyes again and this time stop talking. What can you hear around you? What does it feel like to put your hands into a bowl of flour and let it run through your fingers? And after all that, can you remember what it's like to feel hungry? Cooking is about waking up your senses.

How to wake up your senses

Smell

Some smells make you want to close your eyes, breathe deeply and smile – warm bread, melted chocolate, the person you love the most, your pyjamas. If you are hungry, food smells great. And even if you're not, you can generally squeeze something in if it smells good enough. When you're cooking, use your nose before your mouth. Can you tell by the smell that you need more salt or sugar? Can you tell by the smell that some fruit will taste good or that some fish is fresh? You will be able to, if you follow your nose.

Taste

Think of the television advertisements about food. They're all about persuading us to taste things. And the moment they land on our tongues we'll be whisked away to an imaginary land of milk chocolate and no school. Taste is about four sensations – sweet, salty, sour and bitter. They're like the colours in a painting as well. A little more or less of each builds up a taste that's good enough to eat. Food doesn't always taste as it smells. So always taste everything as you're cooking and, together with your nose, you'll learn how to turn a good dish into a fab one. When the recipe tells you to 'adjust the seasoning', it means using your taste to decide whether you've got enough salt, sugar, spice or bitter flavour in your dish.

Seeing

How often have you looked at a plate of food and thought 'That looks like a heap of horribleness?' What we see on our plate makes all the difference to whether we want to eat it or not. It's the same as when you're cooking. Always watch what you're doing and especially watch what's going on in the saucepan or oven. If you take your eye off the ball you could end up with a heap of something nasty. You also need to use your eyes to watch what happens to food as it cooks. Potatoes start to look soft when they're cooked. Cakes and biscuits go golden or brown. Onions begin to look see-through and change colour too. The more you watch the food as it cooks, the better judge you will become.

Hearing

There's a reason why so many people eat cornflakes. It's because when you pour on the milk they really do crackle. What you hear in the cooking pot or the kitchen is also important. Drop a cube of bread into hot oil and you'll know by the noise when the oil is hot enough. It sizzles. You can hear something boiling because it bubbles loudly. Make sure you can always hear the timer. You'll always know when something is cooked through because it sings in a sort of quiet, fizzing voice!

Feeling

This is about lots of things when it comes to cooking and eating. It's about texture. Think of the foods in your mouth that feel hard or soft, slippery, soggy, hot, nutty, sharp. The way food feels in the mouth has a lot to do with whether people think they like it or not. Some people like oysters because they slip down their throat. Others like gob-stoppers because you can't get rid of them. If something you've just cooked feels right then it's probably because it tastes, looks and smells right. Cooking and eating make people feel good. Tasty food is satisfying, warming, pleasurable and, most of all, really good for you.

Index

Acknowledgements

Thanks to Fiona MacIntyre and Penny Simpson
at Ebury Press for listening to us

Thanks to Iain Lauder at Redpath

Thanks to Sophie Dow, who introduced us,

and thanks to our families for eating countless
variations of Easy Peasy dishes